PIECES OF US

THE RISE, DECLINE AND FUTURE
OF A
WELSH NEIGHBOURHOOD

Rob Sheffield

Print ISBN 978-0-9568031-8-4

Published by

Llyfrau Cambria Books, Wales, United Kingdom.

Cambria Books is an imprint of

Cambria Publishing Ltd.

Discover our other books at: www.cambriabooks.co.uk

Dedication

To Joyce, Don, Paula, Ella and Cormac.

Acknowledgements

In April 2019, I started to meet residents from Greenhill and ask questions about the place and how it was to live there. One person led to another: *You should speak to so and so. They used to live on such and such a street and here's their number and mention me...*

Between March 2019 and April 2021, I interviewed 44 people, many in-person, and some online during the COVID-19 pandemic. Everyone I spoke to was interested, curious and glad to have an opportunity to say something. Thank you to all of those people, (some are no longer with us). And to their friends, neighbours, sons and daughters, for easing the way.

The names of all the people I interviewed are changed in this book. The only unaltered names are those mentioned who contributed to the stories and fabric of the neighbourhood. Any spelling mistakes of names are mine.

Many people helped with this book. Mary Clare Pitson helped me speak with people in the locality. Gerald Gabb directed me to relevant, local Swansea history. Thanks to Richard Bolden at the University of West of England, Bristol, for funding the transcription of interviews. George Morgan produced the two book maps, and he worked with Ella Sheffield to design the cover. The hands image comes from the work of sculptor, Mandy Lane, https://mandylanesculpture.wordpress.com/, photographed by Bill Taylor-Beales, www.hushlandcreative.com, and shared by Cerian Appleby, from St Joseph's School. And thanks to Camilla Watson for sharing her community work project in Alfama, Lisbon.

I benefited hugely from writer friends who read and gave me useful comments on a very rough first draft. And thanks to Chris and the team at Cambria Publishing for making the publishing process straightforward.

Libraries helped a lot. I researched about Greenhill, Swansea and Wales in the Swansea Central Library and the National Library of Wales in Aberystwyth. And I drafted the book in the Central and Gloucester Road libraries in Bristol, and the library of the University of West of England.

Most of all, thank you Rachael, Ella and Cormac for giving me the time and space to work on this, and the love to keep it going.

Contents

Map of Greenhill: 1938

1 Red Cow
2 Bluebell Inn
3 Malsters
4 Old Duke
5 Full Moon
6 St Joseph's School
7 Social Club
8 † St Joseph's Cathedral
9 Brynmelyn Park
10 Swansea Railway Station

Map of Greenhill: 2023

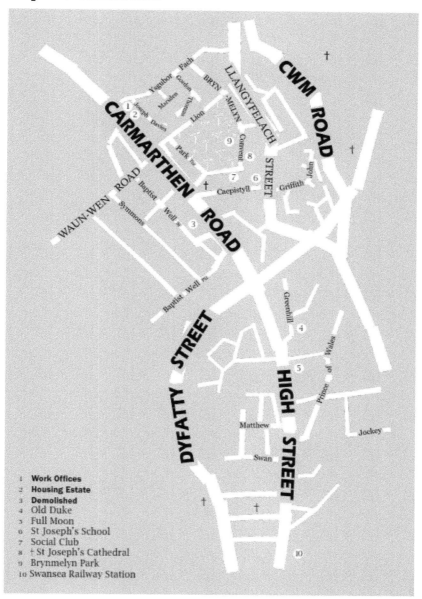

1 **Work Offices**
2 **Housing Estate**
3 **Demolished**
4 Old Duke
5 Full Moon
6 St Joseph's School
7 Social Club
8 † St Joseph's Cathedral
9 Brynmelyn Park
10 Swansea Railway Station

Part 1: Becoming Somewhere

1: Urban disturbance

Arriving by train at Swansea railway station most people turn left at the exit, heading south-west to the city centre, perhaps the beach, or the long arc of the Mumbles. If, instead, you turn right and walk north along the High Street, in 10 minutes you'll be treading the old neighbourhood of Greenhill - a defiant lip of land on the city's ancient slide to river and sea.

Its Wikipedia page describes it as suffering 'some loss of identity for this once very densely occupied part of Swansea'. Identity is not the only change. Ask people from across the generations, and they will offer their singular memories of the place, describing how physical and social centres of gravity have shifted in streets changed or now gone.

Some ascribe the name 'Greenhill' to the Irish influx from the mid-1800s onwards. Roger Price called his 1992 book of the area *Little Ireland*. But the name Greenhill is older than that. Thomas Baxter's 1818 drawing shows the area's pre-industrialised pastoral location, near to, but separate from the town's main living centre around the High Street and the city castle. And, in reference to the 17th century English civil war, an 1878 newspaper reports that, while Cromwell's army were entering the town from the south, 'the king's soldiers were retreating through Greenhill gate'. (1)

The area was certainly green before the Irish arrived. Imagine landing on Swansea beach in the early 1700s and seeing the coastal plain surrounded by hills, carved through by river and streams. If you followed the broil of human activities, you'd have headed north,

1

passing the city castle and on to the High Street. And you'd have seen green hills everywhere. On the tended fields ahead, levelling off northwards on the partial flat of current-day Cwmbwrla, and rolling downhill, east to the River Tawe, and the nearby area of Hafod:

"Delightful Havod, most serene abode, Thou sweet retreat, fit mansion for a God." (2)

This poem was written in the late 1730s, before the landscape of industrialisation came to Swansea. I shared it with a Hafod-born friend of mine, who laughed wryly. Like me, he grew up here before leaving for university in 1982. These were times of transition, as the city negotiated the meaning and tensions of post-manufacturing decline. Landscape and minds were scarred with the debris of industry. A serene abode it was not.

When I was a child here, the area was poor and working class. It was pre-internet, and pre-massification of university education. It was also, I remember, a cohesive place, where a lot of people knew each other. It felt safe to roam and play, and to feel as bored as any teenager wants. Bored but not scared. From 1966 through to the late 1970s, we lived on Symmons Street in Waun Wen, adjacent to Greenhill. I went to primary school at St Joseph's, and to the church of the same name. And played in the ruined houses, chapels, parks and housing estates, and on the empty fields dotted with subterranean World War two bunkers, stuck in their shadowed moment, rank with urine, home to scuttling rats.

In March 2019, the Daily Mail asked

"Is this the worst High Street in Britain? Businesses in Swansea say they are shutting up shop amid 'plague of drug addicts and prostitutes' with police called more than 1,000 times in one year..." (3)

It describes the drugs, guns, violence and claims that shop owners are closing up because the criminals have won. In the same article, the owner of the White Swan pub is reported as saying:

"I'm giving up. I have tried really hard, but people don't like to come up here as they are scared. Even my friends don't visit. We just do not get protection up here...There is no CCTV. We have prostitutes regularly standing on the street, and there is violence. I saw a guy beating up his girlfriend, and when I tried to intervene he turned on me. The place is just abandoned. I've tried to make a real go of this place, but I've had enough."

And in May 2021, at the top of Waun Wen Road - adjacent to my old street - youths sent burning cars downhill, terrifying locals and chasing away the outnumbered police. (4) The subsequent investigation led to sentencing of youths, criticism of the police response, and efforts by the local community residents to rebuild.

***

My father told me that it was hard to find a kinder place than Swansea. My teenage self was sceptical. What I did know was that when many people know you in a place, it can feel like being raised by an extended family. There was a warmth and a knowing that felt like being part of something bigger. And where people on every street knew you and your people, it could be stifling. I left without a backward glance in September 1982.

I lived in Portsmouth, London, Malmesbury and Bristol. Nowhere approached the social cohesion of the Greenhill of my youth. With time, experiences and reflections, a few troubling thoughts kept returning. What was it about this time and place that had left such a mark on me? Did others think, as I dimly recalled, that it was a time and place with strong ties between people? And that this was both good and bad. And what had happened to this place I once knew so well?

And it wasn't only curiosity. Why did I still feel something that felt like guilt?

Dislodged by all this, I booked an appointment with my local GP. After a detour around my toes she asked: "And you mentioned something psychological?"

"This is a difficult thing…it's about my parents. I left for

3

university, and I didn't really say thank you to them. For what they did for me. And I'm not sure what to do about it."

There was quite a long silence. "You're talking about heartache", she said. And she recommended *The Four Pillars*, by Ranjan Chatterjee.

"I'm thinking of writing a book", I said, without much conviction.

"Don't write a book" she said.

***

In April 2019 I started talking to people in Greenhill about their past and present in this place, trying to understand more. I spoke with local residents, some of whom I'd known from my earliest years. And with teachers, priests, council workers, and political councillors. I worked through samples of daily newspaper headlines from the South Wales Evening Post, and read official documents about Greenhill. And I opened my own diaries and journals from earlier years. Then COVID arrived, closing the libraries, slowing the work, limiting physical interactions between people and making community sharply topical again. And releasing echoes of Greenhill's own past.

2: A place forming

Greenhill has long faced economic vagaries, social inequalities and environmental concerns, and that remains so today. The area is adjacent to, but not quite part of, the old-industrialised east. It's in the Castle administrative ward that includes the modern, developed marina, but it couldn't be further away, economically and socially. And it is within walking distance of the city centre and the shining symbols of Swansea's wealth. Since industrialisation, it has wrestled with the challenge of combining economic opportunities with social advancement and environmental sustainability. Post-COVID, the area faces serious problems with the city's highest crime rates; income deprivation - a net annual household income of £22,000, well below the city's average; and a strong perception that the area has become unsafe. (5)

Its history is of struggle and forming from the opportunities presented by vast, impersonal shifts. One place to start is with the White Rock Copperworks, a 25 minute-walk, north-east of Greenhill. It was established in 1737 by Thomas Coster, the Bristol Member of Parliament, mine adventurer and dealer in copper and brass. Copper ore from Cornwall landed on the river Tawe and was smelted to produce copper products. These would be shipped from Bristol to the Guinea coast in Africa, contributing to the trade in slaves who were taken on Coster's ships to Jamaica and South Carolina.

Copper smelting grew in demand, and the nearby Hafod and Morfa works were built in the early 19th century. From the late 18th century to mid-19th century, Swansea became known as 'Copperopolis', and by 1820 was responsible for producing around 50% of the world's supply. (6) And the population relied on the work - by 1823, around 10,000 of Swansea's 15,000 population were supported by the copper industry. (6)

The spoils of economic growth won over environmental concerns.

Hundreds of chimneys changed the landscape in this area, with the prevailing wind sending fumes of arsenic and sulphur east-ward onto the soil and people of Landore, Bonymaen, St Thomas and Kilvey, killing trees, crops and poisoning pastureland. While workers lived nearby, and farmers lodged court cases against works owners, those same owners lived in the city's west, in the more salubrious Brynmill, Uplands and Sketty.

Rapid economic growth needed new labour and numbers increased steadily in the following decades, as people were attracted to work, producing ingots and sheet copper, yellow metal bars, sulphuric, oxalic and muriatic acids, and sulphates of soda, copper, zinc and other chemicals, as well as coal, artificial manures and fuel. Travel between Ireland and Swansea is centuries old, and as work opportunities grew, Irish immigrants became the largest external source of people for Swansea through the 19th century. This grew from around 400 people in 1838, to 1369 by 1851, and 2800 by 1859. (7) Many settled in Greenhill, in the new workingman's district:

> '…a bleak and bare hillside where roads and streets had yet
> to be made, undrained and unlighted.' (8)

In this nascent mess they were not uniformly welcomed. The same was true for their catholic priests. A young Father Kavanagh had needed the protection of bodyguards from insult and injury, on arriving in the city. But, when the cholera epidemic of 1849 struck Swansea, the same priest turned minds. Father Kavanagh offered his help to Dr William Long. Accounts describe him tending to the sick, washing them, combing their hair, making their beds. And, at the end, giving the last rites, and, when needed, placing the dead into their coffins. (9)

Through the pandemic, the Greenhill area had very high mortality rates, and an 1854 medical report explains why:

> "In Charles street there were in December 1853…about six
> to each room, thus creating a pestilential atmosphere, ready
> at any time of epidemic visitation to liaise the disease among
> these inmates... it is notoriously common…to find one

tenant of a bed ill, with two bed companions, one sleeping at the foot and one at the side of the invalid, while in cases where death occurs, the corpse occupies the room which often serves as living, cooking and sleeping room to six or seven inmates." (10)

Since Greenhill bordered the High Street, the effect on city centre trade was considerable:

"At the height of the epidemic, business in and around the town centre was brought to a standstill. A forbidding, eerie stillness prevailed everywhere, further emphasised by the fact that no church bells pealed out their normal chimes; shops were closed and the local copper works abandoned all workers who were not absolutely needed. It was an enforced holiday which no-one wanted, which cleared the streets of drunkards and induced many people to go to church." (11)

Many of the bodies were buried at what is now St Matthews Church, just north of the high street. After his cholera efforts, Father Kavanagh concludes an 1852 report to the bishop of the diocese:

"Religion improves, particularly at the stations. No hostility displayed, but the people do not like our Faith!"(12)

When cholera arrived again, in 1866, the local authorities resolved to act, and cleared poor housing, including parts of the densely populated Greenhill area, which, once again, absorbed a disproportionate rate of incidence and death.

By now, the area was establishing itself as a neighbourhood with a different identity. St Joseph's church had been established in the locality, also in 1866, but the churchgoers were served by priests from other parishes. It was clear that the growing Irish catholic population in Greenhill needed a priest of their own, and they got one. In his reminiscences, Father Richards describes his appointment as the first pastor of Greenhill, in December 1875. There was a population to serve, and he enjoyed the goodwill created from the legacy of Father

7

Cavanagh and others.

"I found in Greenhill an absence of bigotry amongst the Welsh people, and a good understanding between them and their Irish neighbours, which has been to this day a characteristic of Swansea and its people." (13)

It seems to have been a good match, as he reflects after his first preaching, though the wealthier west-enders of the city fare less well:

"There is something helpful about an Irish audience which I have found in no other. They give as well as take. A fashionable West-end audience listens to you with attention, but rarely look at you, and you know not whether what you say goes home to it. There is no speculation in their eye, no play of feature, no outward sign of appreciation, but a stolid irresponsive acquiescence, consistent with a vacant mind...With an Irish audience, a body of uplifted eyes rivet themselves upon you, promptly giving the electric spark that went from you back to you again. You read in their sparkling eyes, and expressive faces the reflection of your own thoughts, and the response to every tone and shade of your own feeling. This is what I found when I preached my first sermon in St Joseph's" (14)

A lot can be done by a small group of people, and in the coming years, it seems that Father Richards and his helpers made a genuine difference to the lives of local people:

"A few years ago, the main roadway through Greenhill was a narrow way edged with hovels, reeking with vile odours and peopled with beings on and over the verge of Pauperism. Now the thoroughfare is broad, and bordered with new and healthy cottages and shops, wherein dwell a hard-working and fairly contented population...it is largely attributable to the good influences which are at work under the name St Joseph. The Rev. Canon Richards is at the head of an energetic community of Priests, Sisters and school teachers who devote themselves to the work of spiritual and intellectual culture with an earnestness that has already produced good results. Fixing upon a rough and declivitous piece of ground overlooking the Greenhill district, and with a fine view of Kilvey Hill, the town, and Swansea bay beyond, the Catholic authorities have transformed the barren place into a veritable hive of religious, charitable and educational effort." (15)

By November 1888, Father Richards had co-ordinated the building of a new church, with money raised locally and from Europe, an organ from Lord Petre, and stations of the cross donated by a family from Antwerp, Belgium. (16)

There was a swirl of momentum. Infrastructure and institutions were being created, and the land itself being shaped. A distinct urban neighbourhood came into being, and in the coming decades the area began to establish the cultural customs and rituals that distinguished the neighbourhood:

> "A picturesque spectacle attracted a crowded congregation to St. Joseph's Roman Catholic Church, Greenhill, Swansea, on Sunday evening, on the occasion of the annual Corpus Christi celebrations, which comprised an imposing procession around the church composed of little children garbed in white, the local battalion of the Catholic Boys' Brigade, and members of the League of the Cross in regalia, the whole forming a striking scene as the procession—about 500 strong,—wended its way around the stately edifice to the strains of the Corpus Christi hymn, 'Lauda Sion," "Faith of our Fathers," etc. (17)

Through the late nineteenth and early twentieth century working conditions were appalling. A twelve-year-old boy might work a fourteen-hour day, and a furnace-man a full twenty-four hour shift. Women and girls might collect urine from nearby houses to clean the copper sheets. Consumption, typhus, bronchitis and asthma were endemic. And the activity of work itself could be very dangerous:

9

"William Connell, aged 56, of Charles Street, Greenhill, Swansea, employed at Vivian and Sons' Works, Hafod, was admitted to the Swansea hospital on Tuesday morning. It appears that Connell, who was working in the Sulphur and copper department, was tipping a barrel of sulphur into a dissolving tank, when the weight of the barrel presumably pulled him in. He was badly burnt about the body and legs, and when admitted to the hospital was in a serious condition." (18)

And work was also precarious. Should wage earners fall ill, there was little family security:

"On Monday night, a policeman while on his beat through a slum alley in Greenhill, Swansea, found a woman and four little children, aged from 1½ to 9 years, huddled in an outhouse. He had them removed to the workhouse where they are being cared for. It appears a few months ago the husband died, and his widow, being unable to continue payment of rent…" (19)

While the neighbourhood was becoming a viable place to live, its people were dealing with the consequences of rapid, unregulated urban growth. They'd have sought their solace and support from different sources, according to temperament, opportunity and chance. Alcohol would have been a source for some, and there were riots in Greenhill in 1903 and 1905, with pokers, stones and metal raining through the air. And at St Joseph's church on Sunday 21st May 1905, Father Fitzgerald bemoaned the role of publicans selling alcohol on Sundays, as well as weekdays. Add to this the minority that ruined the reputation of the neighbourhood:

"They had 5,000 Irish Catholics, and among them perhaps a dozen or so of thoroughly degraded families – he knew them all – who feared neither God nor man, and consequently had no reverence for the law." (20)

In the ceaseless task of keeping the demons at bay, Priests became important authority figures in the decades to come. Father O'Hare replaced Father Richards, and seems to have wielded an unquestioned authority:

> "...the Greenhill district owed its none too favourable reputation to 'company' that the bank holidays of Whitsun and August always drew together, to be dispersed int the small hours of the morning by noisy and violent internal explosions...Father O'Hare...was always there. Whereas the police were powerless, his appearance was often enough to clear the streets and one of the chief officers of the force remarked not long ago, in speaking of those times, that when there was trouble in Greenhill, Father O'Hare was worth more than half-a dozen policemen..." (21)

***

Creation, work, danger and death - these were the trials and joys of people who were clinging to life and to living. As for the people, so for the growing neighbourhood. By the late 19th century, Greenhill was established as an urban neighbourhood area with a distinctive Welsh-Irish culture. This was due partly to the visible efforts of priests, teachers, and others in formal roles. But it was also because of the everyday work of thousands of local people whose hard work was never recorded but who accumulated a growing power and credibility and established their validity in city affairs. In the decades to come the culture and identity that developed at this time would be further consolidated, further institutionalised, and become 'normal'. There would have been strong social connections between many of the local residents. And considerable pride, as their efforts made the area a place to live, for themselves and their families.

This was the formative time. And this was the local history of which we knew little as children, growing up there in the 1970s. In August 1972, my father took me to see "Zulu', starring Michael Caine and Stanley Baxter. I was 8 years old, and it left a deep impression. Back home, we were told nothing about David Jenkins, an army private and one of the few actual survivors of Rorke's Drift, who lived first at 52, then at 13 Bryn-Melyn Street, Greenhill. (22)

Nor did we know about the remarkable Griffith John, born in 1831 to a copper-working family in Greenhill. His mother died in the cholera epidemic of 1832, and his father to a further outbreak in 1849. In 1855 he sailed for China as a 24-year-old missionary and founded the Wuhan Union hospital in central China in 1866. (It's one of China's largest, with more than 5,000 inpatient beds, and treating 3.5 million patients annually.) He is remembered there through a statue of him placed outside the hospital, and his work has led to economic trade and medical collaborations between Wuhan and Swansea.

In Greenhill, he is also known because his name was used to label a block of flats, raised after a post-war housing clearance that brought conflict, and challenged the community's marked cohesion. In the late 1950s some of the older streets of Greenhill were demolished in a slum clearance, almost 100 years after the previous one. This time round, Anne Street, Brook Street, Charles Street, Emma Street and Well Street were demolished, and many people relocated to other parts of Swansea, including Portmead, Penlan, Blaenymaes and Gendros. And on the cleared ground was built the high-rise flats named Griffith John.

Aside from the human impact, the clearance also shifted the centre of Greenhill. It moved a little north-west, away from current-day Dyfatty, to become the area now bounded in the west by Carmarthen Road, north by Ysgubor Fach ('Small barn') Street, and east by Llangyfelach Street.

And this post-war practice of housing clearing was not limited to Greenhill. In *Before the Roundabout: A Swansea Childhood*, Marilyn Winstone describes a similar occurrence in the late 1950s, just north in the area of Cwmbwrla. Roads were diverted, a roundabout built, shops removed, places to meet erased. And in the 1960s, Cardiff city council decided to clear Loudoun Square, the centre and heart of downtown Butetown.

In Toronto, *The Ward* was a central urban district and had accommodated immigrants from many parts of the world. Early arrivals included British, Scottish, Irish and African-Canadians - many of the latter being escaped slaves fleeing to Canada via the underground railroad. Later arrivals came from China, Italy and Eastern Europe. Rapid population expansion had gradually put pressure on sanitation and living condition, leading to calls for a redevelopment of this part of central Toronto. And the area was gradually cleared from 1946 onwards, through to the 1990s. (23)

In Chavez Ravine, Los Angeles, Mexican-American neighbourhoods had developed land and ties over decades, forming tight, cohesive communities. And, in the late 1950s, the area was cleared of these populations, to make way for the Dodgers stadium.

Also in the late 1950s, in Boston's West End, a housing clearance displaced thousands of immigrant, working class people. The area had become a home to Irish, Jews, African Americans and many more nationalities. (Even Vulcans - the actor Leonard Nimoy was raised here.) It was labelled 'slum housing' by wealthier Bostonians, though this was disputed by local residents. And the city government argued that the development would raise more tax for the city. The exodus led to a long-term distaste for urban renewal in Boston, and an official apology from the Boston Redevelopment Authority in 2015 for the community disruption.

3: Maddy

She'd replied to my Facebook invitation, where I'd asked for people interested to share memories of their time in Greenhill. She'd lived there in her earlier years, up to her mid-teens. And now we're sitting in her home near Swansea's seafront. We don't know each other, but she has plenty to say. Her eyes are fizzing with energy and nous. After establishing whether she knows any of my family - maybe... – she starts to share her memories.

It was a community. It was an Irish community because of the Irish coming over in the depression and that. And, of course, they came over as labourers or whatever. And there was a great Catholic community. There was also a big Jewish community, mind [a]. That was on Prince of Wales Road. There was a row of shops opposite the back of the Palace, a playground - be sitting on the palace steps. And most of those businesses there - Mr Katz, big man, don't know if you remember him - and most of them were owned by Jewish people.

My Grandfather was very close to the Jewish community, he used to dig the graves in Mayhill for them, and he was an Irishman. So, I was brought up in a Jewish, Irish, Welsh community... It just dawned on me: there were quite a few Italians. Either with fish and chip shops, or ice creams.

Well, we played mostly in bombed buildings. There was a place called the Bumble - we used to call it the Bumble, I don't know why it was called the Bumble - and that was John Street and Jockey Street, behind Prince of Wales Road, rows of terraced houses. So, we used to play with a lot of those children, behind, because it was safe, to play hopscotch or skipping or whatever. And then you go on a little bit further and you'd be on the Strand, because it was all derelict,

---

[a] Swansea had around 1000 Jewish people in 1914, it declined rapidly afterwards, with Cardiff becoming the main place of Jewish settlement in Wales. (Paul Chambers, Religious Diversity in *Wales, in A Tolerant Nation* 2015, edited by Charlotte Williams, Neil Evans and Paul O'Leary)

bombed, bomb building materials dumped. Must have been something else, sometime. Opposite was quite a big pipeworks. So we used to play in there quite a lot, how a load of pipes never fell on us I don't know, I think we all had guardian angels that lived there. We had good playgrounds. Then we'd go over the river Tawe then, on the swing bridge and play on that. We had a fantastic childhood. May have been poor but oh, the fun we had. The tricks we'd play on each other. imagine four boys and seven girls. But we did have a hell of a lot of fun. And always there for each other.

We even stowed away one day. My sister, myself and a neighbour's daughter. Well I said to D-, my sister, and B-, our friend, 'Oh David's ship is due in' and we've thought then "Oh, we'll go and see it". So off we goes to the docks which wasn't far, from Prince of Wales Road. I'd seen this boat coming in. Now I didn't know the Blue Starling, I knew what a tug was, but I didn't know what sort of ship. So, in it comes and it was coming back to pick this family up for one child. So we all got on the ship and went off to sea.

We wandered around the ship, nobody caught on for a while that three of us - I must have been ten, or something - nobody realised that we'd stored away on the ship. Eventually somebody caught on. But fortunately, it was only going to Ilfracombe. So, we were taken to the captain's quarters. We had a little telling off. And then we sat at a captain's table. Now, lucky I'd come from my grandma's, we knew about silver and serviettes and what china or whatever. And he couldn't get over that we actually knew how to use the knife, and silver, and work inwards... Anyway, cut a long story short, we had a nice day in Ilfracombe, fetched us back, and my mother was just tickled pink. So, it was headlines in the paper there, wasn't it. And I was the oldest - that was the worst. And I led them astray. Could have been anywhere. Thank God we picked a pleasure boat.

The funniest thing that ever happened to us, thinking back now, ... we'd go for a walk by the bridge, by Sainsburys there. We walked and walked and we ended up, must have been beyond Bonymaen, because we'd never been that side of the river. And when we got to

15

Jersey Marine, we thought we were in New Jersey. Some of us were quite young: 8, 9, 10 perhaps. We must have had a guardian to look after us. I'm a great believer in that: whether it's a relation or whatever. But we found our way home again.

But there was work about, there was plenty of work about - they just had such big families they couldn't cope. I mean my mother coped, it was just hard going, feeding and trying to dress your children. Whatever it might be - getting paper rounds all the rest of it; pinching bits and pieces from the rag store...and taking it back to them in a sack; the chemists and pinching the bottles out of the shed and taking them back the next day for a penny each. But we never took more than we needed. If you want to see a film, if you were lucky, you'd go in for nine pence, about a shilling only. And it would only take three flagons - you wouldn't take any more than that. Only if you need it. That's how we survived. (I'm not gonna be had up for this now, am I?) Not acquiring massive amounts. We'd survive. We didn't have a lot like others. That's a good name for the community: survivors. Because at one time they were all wiped out, weren't they, around that area, with cholera.

Ozzie Vanster was a royal photographer, with the glass slides and a biggish camera. And he used to dress a bit eccentric with a big white, painted hat. And he had his big, old-fashioned camera and he fell in our times. And we lived in a three-storey house, and he had the shop. And he used to cook his food, I remember that, in cod liver oil or something. The smells made me heave. And, poor man, fascinating character, he had all slides of all the years he worked as a famous photographer, glass slides. And my mother was taking him a cup of tea one morning - I think it was my mother, it could have been any one of us - and he'd had his feet in a bowl of icy water. He'd died.

And all his stuff was taken away, I don't know what he'd done with the camera, but the slides was taken away down to the Bumble, below the railway bridges, and buried there. I remember that plain, we used to pull them up, out of the dirt. And I thought it was so sad.

There was another one called Dirty Edie, because she was dirty!

She used to keep kittens down her chest. And she'd go to the fish shop, that fish shop, opposite the Full Moon now, and she'd have bits of fish and put them down her chest to feed the kittens.

I used to buy toffee apples from...the Toffee Apple Lady down there. I believe it was Anne Street. She made toffee dabs in a bit of wood. And then she makes penny toffee apples, which is the little apples. If you were really posh you could have the thrupenny one - we used to call it the Big Apple. We'd be queueing up in the lunchtime then, if you were lucky enough to have a penny.

And there were clubs. So there was the Railwaymen's Club. There's the Embassy club. There was the Lyceum club. There were lots and lots of clubs. St Joseph's, Lady of Lourdes was a very popular club. And St. Joseph's, they'd have dancing on a Saturday night. and entertainment. That was before the bingo came about. So again, there's a big social life there for people. There used to be a bookies on the corner, by the doctors there. They used to go out and put a horse on, the men. And if they won, they'd have a couple of pints. There'd be fights on Saturday night, coming out of the Full Moon. Killing each other until they sent for Canon Mooney. And they would run when they saw the priest coming, at end of pub time. Make sure that it was in order, break the fight up, just threaten them with a shillelagh.

All in all, I couldn't wish to be brought up anywhere better. The adventures. Full of adventures. I was very lucky to live in the history of Greenhill and Dyfatty Street and all that area. I had a loving family and loving mother. My stepdad was good to us. We had a vast playground. And it taught me a lot about life. Safety, taking care of my son, being grateful for what I had later in life.

My brother's settled in New Zealand, he couldn't talk about anything because nobody knew him. And he missed that more than anything. D- says, 'When you are gone, Maddy, I'll have no-one but memories.'

4: Bill

He was a close friend of my father for a long time. He has a sharp memory, likes a story, a song and is playful and mischievous. We're meeting at a café, off Oxford St in the centre of Swansea. He's recounting the years before, and during, World War 2, school-life, and how the church' social club became established.

And in them days it wouldn't do no use walking, back and forth to St Joseph's. But the beauty of it was, in them days, there was no cars about. You could play marbles, more or less, in the gutter all the way down. And I will say then...there was all the poverty. It was terrible. You'd see kids coming to school - no shoes, gyms and lumps of cardboard in their shoes. Bags of poverty. Pre-war. Well, I remember going down there as a kid and seeing it on fire, the school. That was the blitz then.

And then I was evacuated. And I can remember being at High St station as a 7 year old, a gas mask, big label, getting on a train and I thought I was going to the end of the world. And it was down to Llanelli.

Well, the thing about it was, I was lucky. I was born, so they tell me, with a good voice. Another tale now, and this one only happened say about ten years ago… One of my friends, Terry Smith, come home and he said to me, 'Bill, Sister by here, I think she knows you from when you evacuated down Llanelli'. And then, I said, 'Good God, she must have been young and all'. She came over to me, she said, 'Is your name Bill-?', I said, 'Yeah. She said, 'I can remember you singing down in Llanelli and I can remember the song you sung'. I didn't know. She said, 'Speed Bonnie Boat'. Once she said the song I remembered Speed Bonnie Boat: "Like a bird on the wing, over the sea to Skye". When I was evacuated, we had a teacher, then, from St Joseph's, with us - Miss O'Mahoney - and she was our music teacher and she used to take me around, I didn't have a bad voice, in them days.

In them days, a priest was a God, right, you know? I remember...

I'm going to confession...the school confession at St Joseph's...every confession will be full, be packed. And some of the teachers...oh God... We had one, Marky Walsh. Now he used to suffer with a bad stomach or something and he used to be dropping off to sleep all the time. See, we were having, like, bible lessons or something like that, he'd drop off to sleep and used to get one of the boys to read the bible to us. And this one used to do it always, a bloke called John Beard from up the Gors, funny enough. And he'd say things like, 'and Matthew and Mark were walking down Wind Street and they bumped into Charlie Splain's Father...' We'd be weak and he'd be fast asleep!

I remember joining the Boy's Club and what caused me to join it was, in them days, I was living in Brynhyfrydd. I was mad about football and I used to support the team Bryn United - and I can always remember the Saints (*St Joseph's*) and this was the outbreak of the war. And some of them were in their Navy uniforms, just joined, you know? And one of them became a mate of mine after, Nicky Collins, you'd know his sons I suppose. Nicky in his navy uniform. But they trounced this team I used to support. And Nicky, if I can remember right, he scored a hat-trick, and they carried him back down to Greenhill and I went with them. And from there, then, I joined the Boys Club. And it was under the church, in them days, for years. And the bloke who used to take us was a marvellous man, Holley - Willy Holley. He used to take us there and all we had virtually were little games and table tennis, we never had a snooker table or nothing then. But, what it done, it brought us together and all that.

On Carmarthen Road, the California. And we were there one day, now right, and there's the priest then, Father Griffin, and I became great friends of his, he finished down in Waterford. And one day we were down there and we were all going now. He said, 'Where you all going?'. We said, 'Going down the Cali now for a pint', and he said, 'Why don't they have a bar here?'. And at the time Canon Mooney was there and he was 'Ooohh...' about a bar. But anyhow, it didn't really happen then in Father Griffin's time, but he was the one who, I think, mentioned it. Another priest came here, then, Father Finlan, and we spoke about it and we got it - we got the bar. And when we got the bar first, I think it was Patsy Pearce, who kept the Adam and Eve then, he used to get us barrels and bring em' up in barrels. And we used to take it in turns behind the bar...where I learnt to pull a pint.

Down the club they had a marker. The marker was the one who used to look after the beer. He was a bloke called Iron Eddy - he had a plate in his head. Danny Shehan, I think his name was. He was the marker there for years and then this character Marky Kolfer took over and he had TB. And you used to go in there sometimes, and he'd be in his long johns, I always remember. He'd take his clothes off, just be in his long johns...

But the beauty of that then, was from there it started to get bigger. And in the end, it'd be queueing on a Saturday night. Because we had an organist then, we used to get an organist then, one of them was David Alexander. He used to play the organ in the Church, and he also played the organ down the club. And they'd be queueing. My wife, who I didn't know at the time, she used to go...and she wasn't a Catholic, my missus was not a Catholic...but she used to go down there, she said, 'I remember queuing on a Saturday night'. And it wasn't outside entertainment then, it was all from in the club, mainly all Irish songs, mind...I knew characters right down there, Tommy Aldron, used to get up and sing...let me think now...'I've met some folks who say that I'm a dreamer' - lovely Irish song. Jackie Conway, another boy, used to sing, 'The boat leaves the harbour tomorrow'. Danny Aldron used to sing all these ones about' 'The brickie up and down in the lift..'. It's a comical one. He used to sing that. There was a singer then, Christy Maguire, he had a good tenor voice and he used to sing some of John McCormack's songs. And the women then...what's her name...Maguire...'I'll take you home again, Kathleen', and all the old Irish ones. But, oh, it was bouncing.

It was another character, J-, he'd be drinking in the afternoon! Because I always remember him outside The Malsters, the pub on Carmarthen Road, by The California...we were all outside...doing a trick...he said to me, 'Bill, got half a crown?', I said, 'Yeah'. I gave it to him, he showed em' a trick and he went in the pub and got a pint! I said, 'Where's my half a crown?'. And you know what, I found a little diary, back years, and I had in it, 'J- owes me half a crown'.

I remember one, a great bloke, and what I loved about him, Pat Dunvan…I mentioned the football team…what I loved about Pat, everybody wanted to go with the first team, didn't they, all the members. You'd have about 10 in the committee going with the first team and poor old Pat would be on his own with the under 17s, but he was great. And he was the first who always used to say, 'Encourage the youngsters, because they're our future'.

5: Eva

Sitting in her house, near the park, the church and the school. She's the mother of a school friend of mine, and has lived here for many years, knowing many people who have been central to the locality. She is describing times from her youth through to the road widening of the late 1970 - which is described in more detail in a later chapter.

It was marvellous, this place to live, years ago, wonderful neighbours and everything. But then it all went and even the name Greenhill went. They call it Dyfatty now.

Greenhill was from the… how can I describe… You know if you go down Carmarthen Road now there are houses on your left and then there's a patch sort of thing? Then if you took the turn there, coming up High Street, instead of coming straight up Carmarthen Road you took the fork on the right, that was Greenhill, from there up to Convent Street. And there were a lot of these little streets off it, you know? There was Anne Street, Emma Street, Charles Street, Brook Street and Well Street. Looking down High Street now, that was on the left-hand side. And then on the right hand side you had Convent Street, Caepistyll Street and Pont-y-glasdwr Street.

Oh gosh, my Great Grandfather came over, say on one boat, and a couple of months later my Great Grandmother came over. I don't know whether they knew each other in Ireland, I couldn't tell you. But they were married in St Joseph's. But he lived in Llanelli because some of them stayed in Swansea, only my Great Grandmother and Father, and another lot went to Llanelli and another lot to Merthyr. It was mainly started by the Irish people coming over, looking for work. They had to put up with an awful lot. They weren't really wanted, I don't think - you know. And I think because of it they bonded together. And, as I say, if anything was wrong they were there in a minute to help. It was great really. Some people give it a bad name because there were people that used to fight every Saturday, but there was far more good than bad came out of Greenhill.

I lived in Llangyfelach Street. So, you had the dairy on the corner, then you had a bakers, then you had a butchers, then you had Stricks, which was a big wholesale place and fruit and veg shop. And then you had all little shops there, and then you came up to the school. So it was the road between Stricks and the school, where I lived. Those houses are still there.

I mean, with the Church you had the Girls Club, the Boys Club, then you had the Children of Mary and the CYMS (Catholic Young Men's Society), then it was the Mothers' (Union). The CYMS went from 16 to when you died. Each society in the church had a representative on the parish council. M- and I were on it for ages, for years, off and on.

And you wouldn't remember the Corpus Christi processions. We went through town. The Corpus Christi used to come through here. We had about three or four that went through the town, band leading them and everything. And we were waiting in Orchard Street for St Iyltyd's Church people to come across and Morriston Church to come down. And then we all marched down the Kingsway. And we were standing there, H-, M-, M- from Waun Wen Road, we were there now, with our capes, and these boys came up, they must have been in a club on Wine Street for dinner time. One of them said: 'Good God look at the girls - we were with them down the pier last night. They're nuns!' Yes, we used to have lots of fun. It was marvellous, when I was growing up and there was loads going on.

I think it was companionship. It was the main thing. Because, I mean, M- and I now, since school days we've been friends. And all the other girls around. We left St. Joseph's at 11 because we passed our scholarship. M- went to Glanmor, I went to high school. But you'd meet up, getting off the bus by the station, you'd meet and you'd walk home because you'd be on different buses. And, as I say, we all stuck together, all through the years. Everyone knew everyone else.

Do you think the men knew the men as well as the women knew the women?

Oh, yes. Because my father had been in the army, he lost his job

23

while the general strike was on. He had two uncles who were in the regular army. He joined the army but then he came out just before I was born and he ran the boys club, in the crypt under the church in those days. And Willy Holley was my uncle on my mother's side, he and my father ran the boy's club for years. And when the boys went to the army, and my father was in the thick of it then, he was called up straight away, they all came up to the house to ask how my father was. And when my father died, 1969, all the men walked in front of the coffin when they were taking him to church. Yeah, the men were equally as friendly with one another.

Canon phoned myself and M- and said, 'Can you come down this afternoon, I'd like to have a word with you?' And I thought N- would have done something, cos' he was always in trouble. And we went down and he'd said to us, 'I can hear all the boys talking about how they'd got on, and none of them played for St Joseph's'. So we said 'well there's no boys' teams in St Joseph's'. And he said, 'But the men...always had a good team. And he said, 'Do you know anyone who would run it, or runs any team?' Well I don't know if you ever came across John - ? So we asked him would he come up and run St Joseph's and he said, 'Yes alright' and he came up to see Canon and he gave him the money for the kids and then they had 6 teams going. And they still got 2 teams of the colts going and 2 of the mens'.

But, as I said, there were loads of characters around, early on. But people became too posh...when they moved and they had these nice houses, that was it. Because people who moved up, perhaps in the same street, they never bothered with one another.

They've all gone now. I mean, there were two just down on the road. There was The Red Cow and the Bluebell. Then, cross the road, and then you had the Malsters, the California, and as you went down to the lights then, you had the Rock and Fountain one side and The Angel the other side. And, you know, women as well, used to go to, they used to call it 'the snug'. They had little rooms for the women to go in. And, I mean, they'd go as well and have a glass of beer, in the nights. It was just company, I think.

(On the effect of the later road widening) Yeah, there were three fish shops on that side of the road, fish and chip shops. And the butchers, a butchers down there. You had loads of shops, but now there's nothing again. You got the Spar and you've got the fish and chips shop and the Indian, and that's all there is. I used to go down the road every day, every morning I'd go for my bread and have a chat with somebody. I remember Jack being here and saying, 'Oh my God, I could be in Cardiff and back by the time you go down the road'.

6: Joan

In the quiet home of a woman I've known since I was 4 years old. As far as I remember, she has always been living here. She is describing times in the neighbourhood from her mother's days, pre-World War 2, to raising her children in the 1970s and early 1980s, through to the present.

You know, we were all friendly and neighbourly. I mean a lot of people belonged to St Joseph's. Lots of people were in school and sort of grew up together and that made it more of a community. When my boys were here, they knew everybody in the street and they knew everybody around. But that's not like that now. Well, you don't see the children out there, they spend half their lives on phones.

I mean if you ever needed, help, there's always somebody you could go to. There was somebody who would always come. Like my husband died when the boys were young - you know this story, anyway. You know if I needed something there was a chap up there living on the terrace, and used to play with the children. He'd come down and do something - if I needed something he would just ask. But it's not like that now. That spirit of helping each other out is gone.

Instead of doing up the houses, they knocked them all down and built those flats. And they did the same down in Llangyfelach - they had the little streets there, my grandparents were born and lived down there, in Greenhill. But instead of doing up the houses, they knocked them all down and built those flats. And apparently, I was talking to somebody, they moved the people from there up to Penlan, or wherever, and whereas they were always very friendly and neighbourly where they lived in the houses down in the streets down there, all that stopped. They weren't like it anymore when they were in the flats; it was a different atmosphere altogether apparently. But that community would have stayed, but they didn't do it you know. And those flats, they were appalling.

I remember a lady - I can't remember her name at the moment - but she went up to - it was Penlan, or Blaenymaes, one of those estates. And she said, 'You don't see anybody, Joan'. She said, 'You don't see people'. But they should have built the houses before, Robert, not those awful flats. They are soulless and the people there left. It wasn't the same once they took them away from there, and the sort of community spirit had gone. It wasn't there anymore.

There were shops and things made it a community. You know the people and everybody knew everybody and we didn't have to go off everywhere to look for something to buy, we'd just go down the road. There was the shop near your house, Mrs Day used to keep it. I've been in there when I used to go to Lillian's, I've been in there looking, and funnily enough she was always up, out in the other room in the corner, and we had to call her. She'd come into the shop but that was the sort of place, it was a friendlier place. A big thing I think that's sorted out Greenhill and Waun Wen was the dual carriageway (*widening*), I really believe that. Down here we had the butcher's shop, Aiden Williams, and they knocked that down... I mean the doctors surgery was on that road.

My mother would be outside and they knew everybody on the Terrace there and a couple of women from the street, Mrs G- and Mrs B- outside - there would be about 4 or 5 of them talking. I mean they were just chatting. You don't see that now. I remember going across to Symmons Street to Lilian's one day and there was something coming up with the royals I don't quite know what it was. And the lady across the road, Rosie, she was organising something that was going on the next day. And they'd always have one big organiser, there was always one boss in every street. And you'd always get somebody there who'd organise a picnic, take the kids down to the beach and all that you know.

I never went to Spain when I was growing up! I mean I'd never heard of anybody who went to Spain. They used to have, they'd have a bus, somebody would organise a bus, everybody got on the bus and pay what have you, when they had to pay and we'd go down to Caswell. And you know we thought it was marvellous, lovely. Now they didn't go to Spain or, you know, Majorca or anything - it's unbelievable. And Disneyland. Nobody ever went to Disneyland!

Most of the people around were all church goers, and they all supported, you know financially supported their church…they did things around the Church - not just the religious services. They had the Mothers' Union and all these things and they all went on trips. I remember my mother you know they used to have an outing every year - they used to go to Jersey or something like on a holiday and they all went. It wasn't only supporting the religious services - they did that, but they did other things as well.

I mean before St Marks was knocked down, they couldn't even afford to pay the electricity bill. That was a thriving church it really was. And I mean it was a very, very popular little church and lots of people from around here went there, but then it sort of, I don't know when it was, because people moved away or whether they just stopped going, I don't know. But I know very well they couldn't support it - they had to let it go. And they built flats there and knocked it down.

7: Tom

A school friend told me about his uncle, Tom. After a few weeks of trying, we finally talk by phone. We spend some time sorting who we know from each other's family. He knew several of my uncles and my father. He grew up in the area in his youth and married years, but moved away some years ago.

I was actually born in Baptist Well St. I got married in 1970 and we moved into Neath Road, just on the bridge there, by the Dublin. And there was a flat there so we took that flat for about 7 or 8 months, it wasn't very nice, the roof leaked like a sieve. And then eventually a house became available in Baptist Well Street. And we had an auntie who lived next door. She wasn't a bloody auntie but we called her auntie. So anyway we made an offer and we were successful, so we moved in there and yeah that was nice. We were a young married couple. In the street I grew up in, not ideal by any means but it was convenient so we stayed.

It was a great little street I knew everybody in there. Everybody knew my wife - there was a little shop there that she and her friend worked, so everybody in the neighbourhood knew her, she was right at home. We were a lot poorer, I reckon, in those days you know, and they had to make do with what they got and they relied on people. It goes back, you've heard this a million times I'm sure, that doors were never shut at night. People trusted each other, that generation that had come through the war. And a lot of the men didn't come back, I guess...But people had to pull together. You had put fires out in each other's houses; you got to see people, warts and all. But anyway, everybody had each other, so to speak. There was a lot of trust in the area between families.

People would help each other, looking after each other's children, maybe sharing clothes. I mean they'd be sharing hand-me-down stuff. They'd be sharing furniture. I often remember, with not a small degree of shame, that I mean we were pretty poor ourselves. My father was basically a labourer when he came off deep sea, he was a deep-sea sailor during the war, in the merchant marines. And when he finally came ashore he was just labouring. He had no skill as such. So there wasn't a lot of money to go round. If somebody had a couch they didn't want or something like that well my mother was only too happy to take it. Because we were kind of rough kids and we'd destroy anything in 20 minutes flat, you know.

It seemed to be a matriarchal society in a big way you know, when I was growing up. Because maybe the war had taken a lot of the guys. A lot of the guys that come back from the war were suffering from what they call PTSD now these days. I don't know… Women had to be strong. My father had a hell of a time - he was torpedoed twice in the north Atlantic and the boat blown out from under him. So, he wasn't the man he used to be when he came back from the war.

Religion didn't have that big of a say in the matter. It did have at one time of course - I mean everybody was anti-catholic at one time. But hey, those days, thank God, had gone, mostly anyway. Poverty more than anything, I think, pulled people together - more of the circumstances.

When I was growing up as a kid Greenhill was starting to be demolished, thankfully. But I remember the dust-tip down there and it was a refuse tip shall we call it. Right next to where people were living, and all the problems that come with the rats and everything else. And it seemed that the powers that be, who put it there originally, had no problem dumping their crap around the catholic community - which it was at that time - very much an Irish catholic community. So that was still there, I remember the houses becoming empty and people moved up to Penlan or Blaenymaes, or up the Gors, Townhill, Mayhill. And I would say it was a good thing. The people's standard of living improved dramatically.

But come the time, the 70's I think, most of that had been demolished. We used to go in there with some friends, we'd go in and smash up the fire grates and take them to Jimmy Shaddick - the scrap man, and sell them for scrap. And the men who did that for a living, the real scrap merchants were not happy. They'd beat the shit out of us, if they caught us. But we used to make good money for that. There was a lot of make do and mend going on, and a lot of people scratching by.

And of course there was always the demon drink. The place was full of fucking pubs - excuse my French. And when the stresses of their house and the myriad children got on top of people, for a couple of pennies at one stage you could go to the pub and meet up with your mates. That's one way of looking at it I know but also those pennies might have been invaluable in the house, so it's a double edged sword. Everybody knows the stories of the drink are infamous among the travelling Irish or the Irish who lived from home. We are a morbid fucking bunch and once the drink is in them…they tend to get drunk and die in the gutter, or locked up or go to jail or killed or whatever. Until usually some woman rides to their rescue. I don't know if you would have seen much of it in Symmons Street but yeah along Bryn-Melyn Street, and places like that, where they'd get roaring drunk and fight in the street and all that stuff.

And the women were as tough as the men… yada, yada, yada. It's all true actually. They could fight as hard as the men. And the teacher who came up to the Boys' school. Yeah, he hit the boy across the face with a cane. So, he lost his rag and hit this kid in the face with a cane. And the mother came up and laid him out.

They were tough fucking kids that's for sure. But they had to be tough because they grew up in a tough environment. And then they had to go back home. Life, you know, and what you see in the home that makes you so tough and hard. How many times have you been beaten up and what caused it? Was it poverty caused it or the drink? I guess we can be thankful there was no drugs around and such at the time. The booze was drug enough. Because people were living in poverty you know, and it grinds you down. There's no doubt about it.

31

8: Pieces: The 1930s to the 1960s

Priest 1: I remember him telling me, and he wasn't deadly old then, going to school in his bare feet. I just couldn't imagine. I met many people, then, after that, who were telling me that they went to school bare-footed, and the stories of Anne Street, Emma Street, Charles Street, Brook Street...it's like the litany of Greenhill, I call it.

Mia: There was only me, Vera, Joyce and Billy then. Sheila and John wasn't born. We're talking about, I was 4 - 80 years ago... And I can remember being in the shelter. And Auntie Maggy was there, Clifford, in the back now, in the garden. And there was an incendiary bomb, I think it was, that bombed the house. And it blasted the shelter down. So they are there to dig us out. And I can remember Jones, Auntie Lizzie's boy - what was his name? Glyn! Glyn Jones, carrying me on his shoulder. And when I looked, the house was on fire. And they took us over to Cwmfelin works. And we were all laying on the floor in Cwmfelin works...

Priest 1: There were the guilds...what they call guilds...religious...the guild of St Agnes...the Children of Mary. These were run by the nuns. Which were religious, slash social, gatherings. Again, it was the church that provided the recreational life of the children, such as it was.

Katy: Men used to go out on the trawler doing fishing, and they'd come back in with big bags of fish. 'm going back now, war time. And there was one man opposite us, used to bring back the fish and he'd give my mother the bag of fish because his wife didn't like cooking fish, but my mother would cook all the fish, and then give them some of the fish as well. Their names were Gibbs. And his son now, I don't know if it's his son or his grandson, I'm not sure, but he's a taxi driver, and I was coming home from Tesco's one morning in a taxi and I said 'Oh your name is Gibbs'. He said 'Yes'.

And I said 'Oh I said I remember Mr Gibbs living opposite us in Colebourne'. And I think he said 'That was my father' you know. And how funny that was you know because I had known them as little, tiny children.

Priest 1: Going back to the days of the girl's club and the boy's club - which I believe Canon Mooney started - there was a strict segregation between both. Each of them would have a holiday down at Pennard, where they had a building down there...a recreational building...which I was reading today, got burnt down, eventually, in the 50s...But it was strictly, you know, girls and boys separated. And I remember someone telling me that Canon Mooney caught one of the boys talking to one of the girls outside the convent one day and gave them a real ticking off. So, that person said that they were very surprised that there were any Catholic marriages because they were discouraged from having any contact with one another.

Church Support: When I was in school a long time ago now, (I can't remember when I left - '59 I think I left school), it was only the local children. And then some came down from Townhill, and around and about. Nowadays, they're bused in from Clase, Penlan, you know. But it was only the local families, and we knew everybody, you know. All the young children.

Priest 1: I remember Mrs - telling me, one of the stories: there was a supply priest there, and, if it had been a regular priest he would have known what it meant, but someone came to the door with a crumpled up piece of paper, and when they opened it is said: 'Can Nora the Flea have a mass for Danny the Crutch?' ... And he said: 'What is this, is it some kind of code or something?' Nora the Flea was one of the characters...and Danny the Crutch was another one of the held nicknames.

There is a story that Father Lenane, who was a much-revered Priest...there was a story that one of these whistling bombs was coming over and there were witnesses to him falling down on his knees and praying. They saw the bomb go down and go in somewhere, but they never found it. It was one of those, you know,

33

stories.

Penny: *(Talking about life for women.)* Not very good. I don't think. No, it wasn't very good for them. The men used to drink. There was nobody hardly working there, was they? The men used to drink. Well, a lot of the men would drink their money. They'd be drunk all the time. And they'd sell their food vouchers. They had food vouchers at one time. Nothing else, no other benefits. And they'd sell their furniture. Mam bought loads of furniture often because Dad was working.

Off?

Neighbours! Well, you imagine having no money - what would you do?

Katy: Yeah well, um, a lady used to live opposite us in number 50 in Colebourne Terrace. Now her mother lived in number 1 Anne Street in Greenhill. And she was called the Banana Woman because she always sold bananas. Then there was another lady down there who sold toffee apples and she was called the Toffee Apple Lady.

Priest 1: Some feel it was a deliberate effort...they wanted to clear what they saw as an Irish ghetto, or a Catholic ghetto, possibly. But, I mean probably the houses in some of them needed to come down. And yet, when you look at ones of a similar age that are still there that have been renovated...

Kevin: ...if they had actually developed the community as it was going along and kept some of the people in the community there whilst they were developing, I think the character of Greenhill might have stayed on. But I think once you move an entire population and flatten that area and then rebuild it, then you've lost that forever...

Vince: I think terraced housing could be - the way they are set out can help people socialise, you know. You can't really socialise in blocks of flats. They just put people up in flats and I always think when they put those up they killed the community spirit because they demolished Charles Street, Emma Street and places like that. I was told that they even lost space, and the council said it's slum

34

clearance, but some residents said 'It's all a load of rubbish and they could have redeveloped the places and kept the houses'.

Kevin: …my honest opinion is that they should have done probably some bit at a time. But I can understand they wanted to get rid of the eye-sore which was these, you know, 2 up 2 down, and lavvy at the back. Get rid of them and you know have real nice places to live. But when you do that you lose the community. It's a difficult choice to make and I think one of the choices, I suppose if I'd been in a position at a time, I would have looked at all the scenarios to see whether we can do half and half, but they decided to do as they did, and I think actually broke the spirit of Greenhill.

9: The wreckage

After almost a century of consolidation and stability in the area, the housing clearances in Greenhill of the late 1950s demolished more than bricks. Many strong bonds that had been created were ruptured, and shared social and cultural practices were threatened. But at the time, little was known about the long-term effects that came from breaking tight, working-class communities.

Dr Marc Fried was a psychologist, looking at the effects of so-called slum housing clearances, as people were moved from areas where they'd built lives and relationships. In the United States, while bulldozers demolished Boston's working-class West End, he took the opportunity to lead a research study on the human effects of urban renewal. After the clearances, Fried concluded:

> "for the majority it seems quite precise to speak of their feelings as expressions of *grief*." (24)

Fried considered it essential to understand the meaning which the area had for its inhabitants. While this notion sounds common sense now, it was not shared widely at the time, nor was it common practice. He highlighted two points:

> "On the one hand, the residential area is the region in which a vast and interlocking set of social networks is localised. And, on the other, the physical area has considerable meaning as an extension of home...This view of an area as home and the significance of local people and local places are so profoundly at variance with typical middle-class orientations that it is difficult to appreciate the intensity of meaning, the basic sense of identity involved in living in the particular area." (25)

Fried's work and other studies showed the integrity of the social and spatial setting in urban working-class areas. Altman and Low called it 'place attachment" – how people connect to places, create bonds, and the effect this has on forming our identity, our perception and our practice. (26) In Boston, people in the study were affected precisely because their social ties and historical attachments were so connected with the specific place. Fried recommended providing continued attachment to place for similar communities in future, whenever residential areas are being renewed. He was a psychologist crossing boundaries into the sphere of housing. When he died in 2008 his daughter said of him: "He was a rebellious, renegade spirit, probably from the beginning of his life." (27)

Part 2: Being There

10: Growing up: 1970-1975

In the early 1970s, while we kids lay in heather and played kiss-chase, the main thought on parents' minds was paid work: getting it, the fear of losing it and fighting to keep it. In the pages of the South Wales Evening Post, work strikes gave journalists easy copy. In 1970, the dockers took strike action, as did Rhondda busmen, refuse workers, sewer workers, ambulance workers, coal miners, school caretakers and cleaners. The power shortages of 1972 produced memories for a generation, sitting at home with family in the ancient, candle-lit dark.

Much of the battle was fought by direct appeals to the public. "The Plain fact is that Britain is up against a rapidly increasing tendency to strike first and talk later", said Robert Carr, Conservative Employment Secretary. At the same time, his government was introducing the Industrial Relations Bill, which sought to introduce tighter controls on union registration and membership, all with the potential to limit collective union action. And when Swansea's 1600 transport and general workers union (TGWU) called off their 5-week strike on Friday November 6th, 1970, they planned to be back at work the following Monday. They'd start boilers and clean classrooms and re-open schools; Swansea market and streets would be cleaned and re-opened, and graves dug again at cemeteries. And Brin Rees, Swansea's strike leader thanked the people of the city for sending the Union many messages of support.

The 1971 Industrial Relations Bill aimed to formalise strikes, limit what constituted a legitimate strike and to channel discussions through union leadership. It was bitterly opposed, and probably contributed to the Conservative government's loss at the 1974 election, after which the legislation was repealed. Strike levels continued through the 1970s, and into the early 1980s. There was action from postal workers, car workers at Ford and British Leyland, blast furnace workers at Margam, schoolmasters, construction workers, British steel, tinplate workers, 1200 engineering workers, ancillary workers at Morriston hospital, British rail maintenance men, and Neath bus drivers. 1600 British steel craftsmen walked out when 2 workmates were sent home for refusing to work on blast furnace 5.

The miners' strike of 1972 involved 280,000 people and 289 pits. 36,000 Miners voted to strike on May Day in 1973, following the "militant line" at their March conference. The term 'Militant' was used a lot in the local newpapers at this time. It seemed to cover collective action plus inconvenience for others. Tall poppies getting above their station and doing things. "Showing off", some people would have said.

With strikes came blockades of products, and enterprising ways around this. "Fifty Militant farmers" blocked beef from Ireland, and 1400 lbs of tomatoes were airlifted from Jersey and Guernsey to beat the dockers' strike in August 1972.

Work was shifting from manufacturing to service provision, and union membership growing for 'white-collar' workers. TV technicians, lecturers, and full-time staff at Swansea student union all went on strike. The latter opposed their own students' vote for greater bilingualism in union affairs, because it would cause an unacceptable increase in workload.

There was a strong culture and organisation of collective action at this time. People went on strike for pay rises, back-pay, protection of rights, working hours, safety, and to protect their fellow workers. Safety in numbers was a great psychological support against the generalised fear of the abyss.

The pages were full of contracts and jobs won and lost. There were redundancies at Imperial Smelting, and 1120 would lose their jobs at Newport's British Steel plant. The Swansea John Lewis store, open since 1866, would close on December 6th, 1975. 62 part-time and night shift women would lose their jobs from the toy manufacturer,

39

Mettoys. The docks area was recovering after the miners' strike, but the effect of the 3-day week was being felt through the supply chain. New contracts were promised at Alcoa, the US aluminium plant; a new dry dock would create 2400 jobs at Port Talbot; Cam gears landed a £6 million contract with Ford of Europe to supply steering gear units. The decision on whether to close Brynlliw colliery was deferred in 1974. (In the mid-1970s, 570 men produced nearly 200,00 tons of anthracite. The colliery closed in July 1983.) (28)

Work gone was the shadow in which many toiled. 'Work' was the place where fathers, and, increasingly, mothers, did what they did. Work was over there, and home was here. Work was an 'other' - an unreliable companion, a sprite. It may disappear without warning, leaving finances in grim straits, and had to be guarded against. And work could be systemically debilitating. Black Lung Disease, or just Black Lung, is an occupational hazard in coal mining, and when the Coal Board introduced the Pneumoconiosis compensation scheme, some 39,000 miners and 150,000 widows across the country were expected to benefit, with payments up to £10,000. (29)

More women were working in this time. According to the UK Office for National Statistics, the employment rate for women, aged 16 to 64, was 52.8% in January 1971, and 56.9% a decade later. (It's climbed ever since, and was 71.6% in January 2021.) (30)

∗∗

Money worries also meant re-use, minimal waste and enterprise. It was a make-do and mend time and place, a circular economy before the term became popular. My mother was a seamstress, and after cooking each day's 5 O'clock 'Tea', of chips with beans, or fish fingers, or corned beef, my sister, Paula, and I would see her 5-foot frame and still, calm eyes, bent over her black and gold Singer sowing machine in the corner of our living room, beside the coal fire's brass guard. Pressing the foot pedal in a rhythmic whirr, and summoning the steady sound of a large dragonfly's wings: ffffrrrrrvvvffffrrrr... She'd be repairing clothes for friends and family. Sometimes for free, sometimes for a little money 'on the side'.

As Paula and I were able to get ourselves to school, so Mam took more regular part-time jobs, including one with Terry Francis the tailor at 54 Walters Road in the Uplands. Along with the equipment, she had the skill and the temperament for this detailed, fine work. Mam was an introverted soul, keeping her thoughts to herself, occupied in her mindful thrum.

The small ads in the South Wales Evening Post show that 7 blood oranges cost 10p, a tin of Heinz custard was 13p, and "London Prices": could be had for gold and silver sold at Stations jewellers. Other ads requested "offcuts from squirrel coats" and, disconcertingly, one promised food that was "similar to kitty cat".

Near us, several people had shops inside their homes. On Skinner Street and Baptist Well Street, and on Waun Wen Road, where Maggie Day's shop was the front room of her house. She sat in the rear room, with her quiet and kind husband, Tommy. We'd stare at the shelves of boiled and sugared sweets in jars, and ices and lollies in the fridge freezer: lemon, vanilla and raspberry bon bons, twirled aniseeds, fruit salads, black jacks, frozen, triangular 'jubblies', golden klondike chewing gum in a beige cotton bag, cream soda and limeade pop, sticks of liquorice, criminally stuffed in carboard tubes of fizzy sherbet. And, later, the wildly exotic cabana chocolate bar. And many bags of crisps, behind her door leading up the stairs. In this era before mass travel we encountered many new tastes through Mrs Day's emporium and imagined with dumb wonder the minds from those worlds that combined coconut with cherries.

No wonder teeth were rotting and "deplorable" in Glamorgan. Only 8% of school starters had perfect teeth. In a typical child's mouth, 6 teeth were decayed and 1 was missing. In a quarter of children, half of their teeth were decayed or missing. "it's the sugar that causes all the trouble" said a later report, in 1974, confirming that Britain has the largest per capita consumption of sweets and sugar in the world. (31) I didn't think of this, as I tasted the gritty, still-sugared chewing gum from the Symmons Street pavement where I'd sometimes lay on too-hot summer afternoons.

41

Dad was the assistant manager at the Alliance Cash and Carry in Fforestfach. Every Thursday, he'd bring home a box of 'fallen-from-the-shelves' goodies. Mr Kiplings' Almond Slices, Cherry Bakewells, Battenburg cake and more. And, most grimly, an industrial slab of toffee, stuffed with Brazil nuts. We waited, obedient and passive, until he arrived soon after 18.00.

**

United Carbon Black made 'carbon blacks', a form of soot for car tyres. And the fine black powder rained down on locals in Port Tenant, making washed clothes dirty, and raising questions about the effect on lungs. Local "militant" mums protested, with a three-week blockade of the plant, a subsequent visit to Downing Street, and threatened to visit the Surrey homes of the business' directors. (32)

For Swansea in the 1970s, sewage was never far away. In July 1974, heavy rains brought flooding to the Sandfields – a flat area of Swansea, beside the sea. Victorian drains, handling floodwater and raw sewage, were unable to cope with the spilling water. "Beach Children play near foul sewage outlet", said the headline on 30th July 1973. Children on the Gower's Oxwich bay were making sandcastles near an outlet designed to carry surface water, that was now polluted with sewage.

And while 60% of people surveyed wanted the city's main foreshore to be developed, pollution in the bay simply had to be improved. And sewage was a major contributor, with 40% of it being discharged directly into the bay without receiving any treatment. Affluence and effluence were uneasy companions.

As children, we would run the great gap between high and low tides on Swansea Bay, tip-toeing disgustedly through the grey muck we called Granny's Custard. We were sure it was oil leaked by local industry, (though it may have been lake or estuary mud from an earlier age).[b] And when we reached the glorious brown-grey water, we were

---

[b] Swansea University geography professor Danny McCarroll said: "There are

42

joyously free, and nowhere could possibly be better. Until, aged around 12, and swimming aimlessly, I swallowed a mouthful of Swansea's finest.

While economic growth and prosperity required a clean-up, older terrors of disease were never far away. Visitors to the Gower are causing a typhoid epidemic risk, said D. F Tucker, a Gower Engineer. They'd been seen peeling potatoes and other vegetables in the public lavatories. Food and loos don't mix, and the sheer number of visitors was putting pressure on the sewage system. (33)

Diseases brought by 'others' was an old fear. Swansea had built trade links with Cuba to support the copper-smelting industry. And in 1865, the city became the site of the UK's only outbreak of Yellow Fever, when the Hecla arrived at dock carrying a cargo of copper ore, and a few, infected, mosquitoes. In the following weeks, at least 27 people were infected and 15 died. (34)

In April 1973, following a smallpox outbreak, London was declared a contamination zone by the World health authority, and Britain declared an infected area. Swansea was preparing for further outbreaks, and Boots stocked vaccines in readiness. And in October 1975 workers at Milford Haven were not sure if they could stop rabies-ridden dogs from entering the country. Rabies was becoming a growing threat, according to the government and the tabloids. The rabies-thermometer maxed out in 1976, as the World Health Organisation said that the disease was advancing 20-30 miles westward each year. The focus seemed to be on France and dogs, which was strange because no-one had died from a rabid dog bite in France since 1924, and the disease was more widespread with foxes.

---

deposits in Swansea Bay, but 'petrified' is not quite the right term. There is a buried forest there that grew when sea levels were lower, and is mainly oak and hazel…The very sticky mud will be lake or estuary mud that formed about the same time." (https://www.walesonline.co.uk/news/local-news/truth-grannys-custard-forest-used-15702927)

Anyway, the clear message was that strong borders were important, and the UK must keep its nerve at the prospect of invasion.

Perhaps the real point was Britain's independence. After two failed membership bids, on 1st January 1973, Britain joined the European Economic Community, and a Union Jack flag was raised at midnight to celebrate the moment of inclusion. This was despite the South Wales Evening post reporting the Confederation of Fried Fish Caterers' Association complaining that British Fish and Chips were endangered because the European Economic Community (EEC) would not allow us to use our beloved synthetic, non-brewed vinegar, which "imparts a better flavour to fish and chips and has a less acrid smell than the brewed malt variety." (34) The term vinegar comes from the French 'vin' (wine) and aigre (sour): sour grapes.

When the UK decided whether to remain in the EEC in 1975, Peter Shore, the Labour Secretary for Trade, visited Swansea's Brangwyn Hall in and argued against Europe. "Have we so abandoned confidence in ourselves and hope in our future...? he wondered. Alas, he spoke to only a handful of people, reported the local news. And the local newspaper had more fun, pointing out that the common market would contribute a £14 million loan to protect steel workers' jobs at Ebbw Vale – the constituency of Labour's anti-EEC Michael Foot. He was unavailable for comment, reported the paper.

Despite patchy support from his senior colleagues, Harold Wilson succeeded, and Britain voted to stay in the EEC by 67.2% to 32.8%. Perhaps the coming bonanza from North Sea Oil contributed. Why rock the boat when the first oil shipment from the North Sea would reach the UK in mid-September 1975, with the potential to reduce national debts, contribute to the exchequer, and help Britain be energy self-sufficient by 1980?

***

In his wonderful book, Ian MacDonald argues that the 1960s revolution was an internal one of feeling and assumption, and changed the West more fundamentally than could any political

44

direction. The 'generation gap' which opened in the 1950s, and was embedded in the 1960s, turned out to be less about differences in generations and more a chasm between one way of life and another:

> "...the sixties witnessed a shift from a society weakly held together by a decaying faith to a rapidly desocialising mass of groups and individuals united by little more than a wish for a quick satisfaction; from a sheltered assumption of consensus, hierarchy and fixed values to an era of multiplying viewpoints and jealously levelled standards; from a naive world of patient deferral and measurable progress to a greedy simultaneity of sound-bite news and thought-bite politics; from an empty and frustrating moral formality to an under-achieving sensationalism...the truth is that the Sixties inaugurated a post-religious age in which Jesus nor Marx is of interest to a society now functioning mostly below the level of the rational mind in an emotional/physical dimension of personal appetite and private insecurity." (35)

After the 1960s, he goes on, this new way of life became so taken for granted that it was adopted by the majority without question. In Swansea that process took considerable time. In 1972, the council voted by 28-12 not to show Danish Blue - the porn film, not the cheese. And in 1980, the city council banned Monty Python's Life of Brian. The ban remained until 1997.

Scanning for moral abandonment was widespread and vigilant. In January 1972, J C K Mercer, chairman of the fisheries committee of the South-West River Authority, wondered whether boys were becoming more interested in girls and pop groups than fishing. Annual applications for children's licenses had declined for the first time, from 4,682 to 4,641.

And Olchfa comprehensive school acted on complaints from parents who worried about communist dogma being preached to sixth formers. It turns out that excerpts from Chairman Mao's Little Red Book had been read at school assembly, along with the bible, for instructive comparison. And a Tory councillor had asked the West Glamorgan educational chief, John Beale to investigate. Not much to report, was the result. (I met Mr Beale a few years later, and he changed my life.)

***

Truthfully, little of this pressed on me. Symmons Street was where I lived, and, along with the surrounding streets, was universe enough. There was no shortage of games to be played and time was of the formal world: an intruder only on late summer evenings when Dad would call me home, to my shame and irritation.

The street itself was full of intrigue. A toad-like man made of circles, stood silent on his doorstep, watching and smiling. A tiny, angry woman, full of corners and sparks and short, angry words, wouldn't give us back our football. And Welcoming Blod, Fierce Doreen and Considerable Rosie. And kind people who did things for us. Malcolm was a carpenter and, one summer, he made pogo sticks for all the kids on the street. For days, a dozen of us bounced along the road, sprung with the sap of our laughing.

Billy was a smiling and genial boxing coach, and he drove an open-backed lorry. He took me, Paul, Ed, Jonathan and Carl, clinging to the frame, screeching through Symmons Street, Skinner Street, Baptist Well Street, Sea View terrace, looking over the bay, then looping back home via Mayhill and steeply down the unforgiving Waun Wen Road. Until the day he told us 'No more', though his eyes were more forgiving.

I had a recurring dream of flight. 'Oh, I'm having this dream again, the one where I fly. Better get ready for take-off...' I'd welcome the dream and enjoy the anticipation of my skill in being able to lift from land. And then the flying itself, as I soared over places I don't remember, though the feeling itself is still present.

It was all about games in a safe zone. Hopscotch, football, marbles, skateboarding, roller-skating, making dens on the rolling hill of

46

Wheatfield Terrace. Cricket - using house steps as wickets. Laying down on the bottle green electricity generator surrounded by bottle green iron railings, that gave strategic views to trouble and opportunities from Colebourne Terrace, Skinner Street, Symmons Street and Wheatfield Terrace. Running and ranging across the heather and hollows of Rockland quarry, with the views down and over the east of the city. Here, at the fringes of our patch, like meerkats, we'd see groups appear 200 yards away, probably from Mayhill, Townhill or Colebourne, giving us enough time to dash home.

And the simple and terrifying Blue Van game. Someone regularly parked a large, navy blue Ford Transit work van on the street. One of us would be a chaser, and others were chased, with all sticking close to the sides of the van. The terror came from never knowing when someone might dash around a corner, only feet from you. And if you took the risk to bend down and look beneath the van for their feet, you may be caught if those feet were moving fast. Unmatched thrills.

Dereliction invited imagination. At one end of our street was a narrow alley, a dose of wasteland, and a ghostly works building. We'd seen enough Scooby Doo episodes not to enter. The already-ragged windows begged to be smashed and we did just that, with stones from the alley below. Sliders, skimmers, bundlers and cubic joes.

At the other end of our street was a disused chapel. One large open space contained pews for praying and service. Beyond, a larger room held a stage and open area for gathering. Here, beneath the side benches we found discarded snooker cues and, under the stage, table tennis balls. Back in the pews, we hid and fired stones at each other from vicious aluminium slings, and imagined we were in a Clint Eastwood spaghetti western. We explored the dark, small side office rooms, where desks and files had once been kept, but which were now dead-still, and home to warm suspended dust.

And, sometimes, when we were tired and wanting divine release, we'd climb from the hill onto the chapel's roof, and lay, cheek to warm slate, mother's milk of geology, where, held by this thin skin,

47

80 feet over hardwood pews below, we'd listen to the birdsong and our own thumping hearts.

***

Ours had always been a football school. And my Auntie Pat tells me I was forever bouncing a football. In July 1974, at the world cup football final, Holland were playing West Germany. Holland, with Johann Cruyff, Neeskens, Johnny Rep and Rensenbrink, playing 'total football' with players seemingly able to play in all positions with equal facility. They seemed unbothered by post-war rationing, had all their teeth, and had clearly been listening to early 70s Bowie. Earlier in the tournament Cruyff had done his famous turn, leaving Jan Olsson from Sweden chasing the shadows of shadows. To this 10-year-old, the right result seemed guaranteed and we were moving to a future where genius would triumph. But the West Germany team was pragmatic, organised and dogged, and they won the final 2-1. The first cut is the deepest and it was a sharp lesson in the merits of stubborn grit.

Sport was becoming a channel for fantasy, and other overseas players caught my eye. Barry Richards and Gordon Greenidge opened the batting for Hampshire. But Richards appealed more. The South African, was the essential oil of easy glory. He was all timing and energy re-direction: flowing, accumulating, easing, composing runs rather than working at it.

Likewise, Majid Khan from Pakistan and the captain of Glamorgan's cricket team. This tough, majestic batsman with the big smile had an ineffable class. Opponents seemed to fall under his spell, becoming subdued and only 70% of themselves.

In August 1976, my father took me to the St Helens ground to see Clive Lloyd captain the West Indies against Glamorgan. West Indies scored 554 runs for 4 wickets, with Greenidge and Viv Richards scoring centuries. But it was really about Clive Lloyd after lunch. Swansea was a very white place in the 1970s, and here was a 6' 4" black man, wearing a white floppy hat, scoring 201 runs in no time at all. Lloyd was liquid energy. He would whip, rotate, flick, lift and place. He'd rarely slash, and never hoicked. As with the best it looked simple enough to repeat.

Music also brought change. My parents' record collection was held in one small box. Ella Fitzgerald, Perry Como, Val Doonican, Sarah Vaughan, Sinatra, Dean Martin, The Kinks, Beatles, Rolling Stones, Get Off My Cloud, 19th Nervous breakdown, Satisfaction, Guy Mitchell and Singing the Blues, Glen Campbell, Tony Bennett. And when Slade came to play in Swansea in 1975, we rang the radio station, Swansea Sound, from Paul's house. Suddenly, we were on air, into the void. We hadn't thought what we'd say, but Paul finally piped up with: 'When's your next single coming out?'

***

Change also came from home. Around this time my mother told me about something from her past. Before I was born, she'd had a daughter, but she had been stillborn at 8 months of her term. The girl's name was Victoria. The news came from nowhere and stunned me.

The medical record from Morriston Hospital says: "1961, Stillborn female infant, Morriston. Pregnancy: normal. Intra-uterine death. Birth weight: 3lbs 10 ounces." Mam was one of four sisters, and one of them, Pat, later told me that my mother had spent months recovering at the home of her older sister, Vera. At the time of the birth, my parents had been living in Vivian Street, Hafod, but the medical record confirms that Mam was discharged to Vera's home in Blaen-y-Maes on 21/3/61.

Once we'd been told about Victoria, we didn't talk about it for quite some time. I never considered that my mother had buried this for the previous 14 years. In 1961, stillborn children were not registered, parents would not have been allowed to hold the child and the child's body was not buried for later visits. The prevailing culture would have said: get on with things and put this behind you. Mam was 29 years old at the time of the death, and she had a large and loving family. They'd have helped her through it as much as possible. Though she wasn't one to share her thoughts and feelings very easily. I imagine her sitting quietly, with Vera being close.

I was born on 1st January 1964. I'd been due on the 18th December, but was two weeks late. It doesn't take much to imagine the anxiety in that room. The birth came after a 28-hour labour which was described as "Apparently normal" by the medical discharge certificate.

We don't know the world into which we're born. She certainly gave me much love, attention, and stimulation. I can vaguely remember a broad sense of bursting delight, through the mesh of my mind's tricks. And the later me can recall the sometimes-presence of anxiety. Of course, for her, it would have been about loss, joy, relief, fear of separation... But she'd internalised all this, placing in her chest a weight that was now a part of her.

Soon after this news, my mother took me to our dentist on Orchard Street, where we'd look from the raised office, down onto the bus stops below, before sinking into the take-no-prisoners plastic, black chair. I must have been having an extraction because the dentist put the mask over my face, said some words and let through the gas. As I drifted away, Mam sat quietly, putting right hand over left, which was on her lap. There was something birdlike and small about her and I'm sure her heart beat fast at that moment. The image stayed with me as I returned, grey-green and nauseous, in the grey-white room.

In the cotton light of my childhood memories, there's a photo-frame of her standing in our Symmons Street kitchen. Her back to the window, warmed by the south-east morning light. Head down, her small hands, busy and precise with the tomatoes, cucumber, the cheese, ham and white sliced bread, Golden Wonder crisps - probably cheese and onion and smoky bacon. And orange squash. She's preoccupied and content, getting together what's needed to take a group of us kids on the number 25 bus to The Slip, on Swansea beach. This was a regular thing: in school holidays, one parent would take a group of children somewhere special for the day. Once, as we headed back from the water to our towels, a friend, Linda, trod on broken glass and sliced open her foot. Her bright-red blood a shocking contrast on the golden sand.

I was both an object of love for my mother, and the source of a silent anxiety. In those years, after a night at the St Joseph's social club, liberated by vodka, she'd return home and plant a loving kiss on Paula and on me, and say goodnight.

Love was felt deeply but said rarely. Perhaps people knew it might be taken away, as with work, and money and homes. Our home radio was in the kitchen, and when 10cc released *I'm not in Love* in May 1975, I found myself lingering on the step between our kitchen and living room, caught in a sonic web. He says he's not in love, but…it sounds like such a sad song… And those swirling, soaring voices in the background, so many of them, so arresting and confusing. Emotions were messy things.

Women were around us constantly. They seemed to be everywhere. Mothers, aunts, neighbours, older girls, talking to each other, laughing, having fun, doing things, being busy, leaning into and part of each other. Women seemed to know what they were doing. And providing food, food, food. If we visited friends' homes, a plate of ham sandwiches on white bread would never be far away. Food as hospitality and food as love. Everybody eats when they come to my house, said Cab Calloway.

***

Men were different creatures. Often by themselves if visible, or, more usually, away at work. In another job, Dad was pounding the car parks of Swansea, collecting the takings for the council. Home around 18.30, he'd sit at the end of his chair, and remove his unforgiving black, plastic, council shoes, and thin black socks. And he'd sigh as he placed his feet in a bowl of hot water. He said it was his favourite moment of the day, and, while he was a natural comic, and loved a Laurel and Hardy slapstick moment, the look on his face convinced me.

Every couple of months, in the slough of a Sunday afternoon, he took me to see his father, on Emlyn Road in Townhill. He held my hand, more than he usually would. Jack sat in what was clearly His Chair. It might have been part of his skin. They'd exchange some sounds between them, but not many. Some of the sounds might have been words, but it wasn't easy to tell. Jack would look at me, with his small, darting eyes. But I don't remember him ever saying a word to me. After what felt like a short duty, we'd leave.

There's an advertisement from the local paper in April 1970. It shows a man smoking a Woodbine cigarette and holding a pigeon. 'Fly what you like, Smoke what you like', it recommends... 'It's not everyone's pigeon, it's yours' (36). Nothing will shift that man from doing precisely what he wants, with his pigeon and his cigarette. That's what the world of men seemed a bit like to me: alone, stubborn and unsaid. A friend who grew up in Carlisle told me that there were only two expressions for male emotion when he was a boy: "fine" and "fucked-up".

With men it might be a head rub, and a sparkle in the eyes. "My handsome boy", said Uncle Len, as he ruffled my hair. I was the better for hearing it. And while I sensed it all around, the emotional world was a curiosity by its silence, and began to occupy my thoughts. I thought that my Dad knew everything. One day, I breathed deeply and asked him:

"Dad...why don't you tell us you love us?"

"I do, of course I do..." his voice tailed off, caught on an out-breath.

I was confused and surprised. I saw the chasm and his struggle to explain. A child can fell an adult with direct words, in a way that adults sometimes fear. And I didn't know then about how hurt and self-protection can travel the generations, becoming habit, character and even a prison.

11: The Place in Youth

By the mid-1970s, Greenhill had been a well-established neighbourhood for many decades. After the shock of the recent housing clearances, the geography had shifted and residents had sought to revive the area and bring some stability. By this time, the institutions of church, school and social club were very well established, and these adjacent buildings were the official spine of the community.

The social club gave an immediate set of pleasures through singing, drinking and companionship with friends. My mother would be there on Tuesdays and Fridays. My father was there most nights.

Many of the children for St Joseph's primary school lived in the local area and walked to school. By now, the school was sending its 11-year old pupils to the recently established Bishop Vaughan secondary school, in the north of the city. Parents took a medium-term satisfaction from putting their children into this good local school, which would do its best for them, bringing a pathway to a decent education.

And for the long-term the church would give ritual, comfort and the acknowledgement of imperfections, through mass, confession, and pastoral support. "Bless me father for I have sinned. It's been six weeks since my last confession. I have sworn. I cheeked my mother and father." "Bless you, my child. Say one Our Father and three Hail Marys."

Together, these institutions provided a triangle of social, psychological and spiritual support from a set of largely benevolent authority figures, all of which brought a stability to the neighbourhood.

Beyond the institutions, there was a strip of nearby, varied, local shops on the Carmarthen Road, from just north of Dyfatty traffic lights, up the A483, on both sides of the road, to the Zoah bus stop south of Ysgubor Fach Street. Hardware shops, grocers, a butcher, a baker, several pubs, hairdressers, a post office, a fish and chip shop, a pharmacy, several sweetshops, and more. These were the places to which people walked, bought the day's food and talked. Unplanned, pleasurable conversations between people who knew each other.

Bryn-Melyn Park was host to long sports games in the evenings after school, and at weekends. Street-life in the summertime was slow and languid. A watery-blue light on waking, and the warm afternoons a muted ochre. And the ground was pitted with kids playing, adults talking on doorsteps, and a few, trundling, prehistoric cars.

Such was everyday childhood life in Greenhill in the early and mid 1970s. Moments were sufficient of themselves, replete with habit and laughter, and rare but stark dashes of excitement and fear. The place where we lived had an insulating property, but events and moments from *out-there* were starting to infiltrate.

12: Morgan

He's invited me into his garden on a warm, breezy spring day. I remember him from my younger days, living just a street or two away, and being a member of a large local family. He's describing the people, the meaning of the place in his younger years, and the leaving of it.

When I was a youngster, before the catholic club became open to couples and families it was just a men-only club. And I remember going down with my father, as a very small child and they'd be playing snooker, billiards and they'd have this little green baize tables where you played darts… And it did have a little bar which just sold bottled beer…I think it was Mr Nash that was always behind the bar…And that was my earliest memory of the club and then of course later on it developed into more of a social club…It was originally it was Catholic Young Men's Society, CYMS, and then because it didn't reflect the age group then it just become the Catholic Men's Society.

Whether people went to church regularly or not, the church was a catalyst. I saw the church as more of a community thing than the religion. Especially with our parents' generation they did meet at the church and then they'd go down the club, they had their drink - which in all fairness to the catholic church they didn't see that as a, you know, demon drink - it was looked upon as part of society. And of course, with all the sort of things that have gone with religion, you could understand why people more or less deride it now, you know. And um, shame in a way because I saw the church as more of a community thing than the religion.

Well, I think going back to the most basic thing was we were all in it together you know. First and foremost nobody went into town, because you didn't need to…I mean our life was lived out in a very small radius, the church, school, the few immediate shops. And then I mean we wouldn't go beyond Cwmbwrla, we wouldn't go beyond the lights. You would very rarely venture down Llangyfelach Road because there was no need to. And Mayhill was another planet…It was like little blocks you know, and that was echoed all round the town I think.

I think most of the pubs then, they wouldn't have seen people from other parts of Swansea, unless they were going to play darts or something else. You know it was like, 'I'm not going to go there - why should I go there? We have pubs here. So because I think pubs play a big part in communities and I think even people that don't drink would agree with that, because they are like a focal point, maybe too much of a focal point to some people but...people would meet there and they discuss things, they get rid of their worries and, you know trying to catch up with the gossip and 'you never guess what happened to Mrs Jones', and all that sort of thing.

And that was it, the social life of these people was, they didn't have to expand, and it wasn't, how can I put it, restraining, it was like they could go anywhere they wanted in Swansea but they didn't want to. They were still happy to go to the Club, go to the Malsters, the California. I mean going to university - it was like going to the moon.

Down the park was a man you didn't mess with because he, I think his name was Mr Pitman, and if you went up and went on his lawns he would be straight down to your mother you know, because he knew where everybody lived.

When I moved from Waun Wen it used to break my heart walking along Llangyfelach Road to go to Landore. Every time I went through Waun Wen, for a long time, it used to break my heart. I mean the place had gone as it was, but I still felt the link you know.

Apparently it's become a little bit seedy. I've heard stories of drugs - well that's everywhere now. With my generation there's still a few older families living there who remember the older days. But, of course, as families move on or die off somebody else comes in and that dilutes the whole feeling of community.

13: Val and Jeff

Val has a wonderful singing voice. One that resonated with me, during St Joseph's masses in my teenage years. After giving coffee and insisting on biscuits, they are describing the social club and the sports life of the neighbourhood in the 1970s, and some of the evolution of the club in the prior years, that paved the way.

Jeff: Well it was Father Finlan really started it as a sort of an entertainment club because that room was called the Finlandia. The main room. From the bar there and he opened it up and took all the snooker tables away, and opened it up as entertainment.

Val: Jeff was steward of the club for three years in the 70's.

Jeff: Absolutely thriving and we were talking about it the other day. It was very popular, it was a like a family club, everybody knew everybody else and they all got on so well with each other. And the entertainment was first class.

Val: Used to be queuing on a Saturday night to get in there to get a seat. We had so many singers there you see, we had so many singers.

Val: But there were so many singers you know and all with these Irish roots. That's the thing you see. All the Aldrons and the Maguires and then your dad, the Sheffields, you know, who had grown up, being in the school. Of course, now the children come to the school from all over. Everybody lived in and around Greenhill and Waun Wen then. We used to walk back and go to school, but they have cars now. They come in buses now.

Now I'm in the choir with people who were in school with me, Pat B- now we were in the same class in school. I mean I'm 82 and Pat is the same. And this is it. A lot of us have just all grown up. But there were so many singers and then they had an organist. We had a drummer for a while but mostly an organist – it was live then, live music, you know. And then they had an organ and we had a few different organists but there was always a pretty good one who would get up and know the singers. And then the whole evening was just, you know just people off the floor singing.

Jeff: It used to be live music at one time and it's not anymore. You don't' get that any more.

Val: But everybody we called up to sing and... It was brilliant wasn't it? It was a really, really good club. There was so much talent there you know. But I mean a lot of the Irish songs, we had friends came over from Ireland - Freda's sister and her husband, an old friend was Freda, and she was a friend of my sisters she was. And her husband, her brother-in-law was a pilot with AerLingus. They still live in Ireland and I get a Christmas every year from them and we send them one and they came over a few times. They used to come over, especially when Ireland were playing Wales in Cardiff they'd come over, and it was St Patricks Day and they came down the club and said: the best St Patricks night they'd ever had. They used to say we knew more Irish songs than they did.

When I was in school we used to have a day off for St Patricks Day and a half day for St David's Day. That's how Irish it was, the community then you see. But the club was thriving and we used to have St Patricks Night, they used to dress up as leprechauns and everything you know. Really good nights.

When I was a little girl, the first time I sang on the stage you know I was about nine. Because my father, we used to go round the pubs, on St Patricks day, we used to have what was called the Irish half hour which went on for two hours, in the hall and my father used to play the piano and they'd make it up, you know.

Bert ran a trip to Ireland. So this was about '84 then, 30 of us on a coach. And we went to Kenmare in County Carey. And we went to this hotel. Bob ran the hotel and Bob had come over to our club a couple of times, and ran this trip right. We had a fantastic trip and in the hotel now he had a sort of Irish band the first night we were there. And we all went into the lounge area afterwards and of course it was such a marvellous night with all these singers that were on the trip you know. Like taking St Joseph's club over there. And it was brilliant. And he booked the band for the whole week. But it got to the thing,

Eamonn Andrews was staying. Do you remember? In the big hotel opposite apparently. And we'd have to finish our evening meal quickly to get into this lounge to get a seat because they were coming to listen to us.

And when we used to go on these trips to Aberystwyth, right. He used to run a trip up to when Dai Jones had this hotel, in Aberystwyth. And we'd go from Friday to Sunday you know. And they'd have a notice up because we all, they'd have this back room then and get a pianist or whatever, and we'd be there then till 12.00 or 01.00 in the morning, having a sing song you know, when we'd go up on a Saturday night, Friday and Saturday night.

(Talking about football in the area.) See and all these then were Jeff's boys that went in, they went in from the juniors then, they went into the reserve division five, and they won it. They won the competition, the first year they were in it.

Jeff: Do you know where I got those boys? I decided I'll run a football team. And I got told these boys were good footballers, about five or six. And they used to go down on a Saturday morning watching the schools playing. And I picked two out of Manselton and three from some other, didn't play in the league. I used to take them training. Honestly, I loved it. I trained them; they were as fit as a fiddle. I come off the pitch after winning, sit down with them in a cafe and give them a pasty, 11 pasties. Swansea senior league, West Wales cup winner, open cup, charity shield, first division runners up and fifth division champions - that was the boys. And I was lucky really, I picked different players and they blended. Oh they were fabulous.

Val: Yeah but you don't get that so much these days.

Jeff: I think it, whoever's running it, they've got to take a lot of interest in it. And they're all individuals, they've got to talk them into doing it. So you can't just talk to them as a team, and say 'come on boys, get on it'. Putting an arm round somebody and talking to them. And that's exactly what's not happening is it?

Val: But, towards the end, that's why the club closed, there were so many older people and they were dying off and all the rest of it, you know. And that was beginning of the end then for the club. Because of course youngsters these days they don't want that sort of thing, they always go into town.

14: Tina

She lives very near where I grew up. Another person I've known forever. She's invited me to visit, and we're in her lounge. It's exactly as I remember it.

Well it was the neighbours wasn't it! There were neighbours then, there are no neighbours now because they're all out bloody working aren't they. It was the women kept the thing going for us, the men were out working weren't they, you know. It's changed a hell of a lot and you haven't got the camaraderie that you used to have, you know.

(I remind her that, one hot summer, her husband made pine pogo sticks for each of the children on the street.)

I know, yes I know. I remember A- came across: 'Are you going to make me one?'

'Yes boy', he said 'I'll make you one'.

So he goes down the back of the steps and I said, 'You'd better make it now - he's waiting for it'.

Oh there weren't much money, there weren't much money. Yeah we were all in the same boat but now you've got the parents bragging what they buy the children and how much you know, and this is making selfish children then innit? I mean I couldn't indulge in mine - we didn't have the money.

Do you remember Mrs Day's shop? Oh God if you wanted to know anything go into Mrs Day's, Maggie Anne Day. And she used to say when she'd see the kids, 'I've had all the chocolates in now for Christmas'. And I'd go over and I'd get what we wanted you know, hide them like because they would have ate them otherwise. But yeah, Mrs Day was a source of information.

We had a beautiful apple tree when we moved in here and they were the big cooking apples you know of course they fell and the kids went over and sold them to Mrs Day. Right well, then they went round the streets selling them again then, she was taking all my customers from me then, oh dear.

Oh me and Ann were very close, very close - Ann across the road. She was a lovely neighbour, a lovely neighbour. And Brian was, mind. And Arthur and Jean. But of course, I don't know anybody else, I don't know anyone.

It's changed a hell of a lot here, a hell of a lot since I moved down here. It's changed everywhere isn't it - not only round here. Nobody seems to want to know about anything. That's the way it is now anyway. I'm not lonely, but it could be I suppose, if I didn't have the family near.

There weren't a lot of money about, but I got to be honest, Robert, we were happier. Oh definitely, definitely. You know, now it's all money-motivated now and they're not happy are they? Well, we were all in the same boat - that's what made it happier. It was nobody better than anybody else because we were all the same you know. But it was a much happier time I think anyway. c

---

c The Gini coefficient measures levels of household income inequality in a country. In the UK, measures started in 1977, and continue to the present. National levels of income equality peaked in the UK in 1978, since when we have become a much more unequal society. Greenhill's poverty would have been spread evenly across its residents and would have been similar to neighbouring communities.

15: Pieces: The Early 1970s

Taylor: I often deny it, but I generally liked that close knit community. I liked the fact that we knew everybody in the street, everybody in the church, and we saw a lot of people - people dropped in and out of our house all the time. I think particularly after my father died...it was quite helpful I think, because, you know, there were lots of things we did - but you know my mother was obviously traumatised by that - that we wouldn't have been able to do with her, you know. We used to go on outings with the altar boys, and all sorts of different groups, and go away with people. The nuns used to come up for tea and we used to go the convent all the time...

Morris: At that time there were 2 sets of Mother's Unions in St Joseph's. You had the Young Mother's which was -'s mother, my mother,....-'s mother, and a big crowd of people like that were one set of mothers. And then people like my grandmother and -'s grandmother and certain other people not so old were in the Old Mothers. It's one of these things that my mum went every Tuesday and they used to have like do's and Christmas dances and stuff like that, and it was very much lots going on. I was in the altar with M- and A- and G- and P-, people like that. And again we went to altar boy practice religiously - boom! - every week on Wednesday and stayed for Benediction. We had trips – one to Caldy island, I remember - and there was a lot going on around there.

Priest 2: St. Joseph's was a very strong Catholic community and the people were proud of their faith. They were many who only came to church for baptisms, first communion and weddings but many who also attended weekly and I presume still do. A few people had difficulty coping with everyday life but had in their own way a deep sense of God in their lives.

Taylor: We were living in my grandmothers' house which was the house my mother had grown up in, and my mother was a teacher in the school, and my grandmother was a cleaner in the school…It was a very caring close-knit community. We were very involved in lots of aspects of it, obviously we went to the school, and we were very involved in the church, and I was an altar boy, and our friends in the street were all in, you know, the Children of Mary, and the Guild of St Agnes, and I was in the Guild of St Steven, and all sorts of things. And my mother was on the parish council and all of this sort of stuff. And I think it was very supportive and we did a lot of things with people in the community. And my mother, your parents went to the social club, and we went to evenings at the church hall, and I was in the drama group and this sort of stuff. So in lots of ways I think it was a very warm, caring, close knit community.

Priest 2: St. Joseph's parish had many Irish families, some were first generation some second. Even on rugby internationals days many members of CMS (*Catholic Men's Society*) would support Ireland even though they had never seen the skies over Ireland. The CMS club was a very popular club. It was opened every night and it was good to go down and have a pint and meet the community, I found it very relaxing.

Priest 1: People used to say to me, 'You've got to have a club, you see. When you have your own parish you've got to have a club, it keeps the parish together'. And I remember thinking to myself, 'No, it keeps the people who like going to clubs together!'.

Sarah: When me and husband split up, Barbara took me under her wing and we were there every weekend, every Tuesday, every Sunday …If she had said to me come down to the club, come to town I would never have attempted it. But because most of us went to church as well - not that makes you any different to anyone else, people going to church - but I did know a lot of them and they were just so friendly. And they were really nice you know and they looked after you. And yeah I felt really at home there and I started going over there then if Barbara couldn't come, I'd go over on my own, and sit with a couple of the women there. But it was lovely, it was really, really nice. It was really the centre of the community as far as

I was concerned…

Katy: Everybody was in the same situation, if you know what I mean…nobody had much more than anybody else. And we all lived that way, well we all knew what each other had, more or less, you know… it made a good neighbourhood then because there was nobody bragging what they got and what they haven't got, you know, and I think that made a community.

Sarah: I mean we'd get up in the morning, I'd go to town and I'd leave my front door open you know. I know loads of people say that now - wouldn't dream of doing that now, would you? Because everyone knew everyone. You wouldn't think of kids running round the street. They're either in school, or I mean in the summer, yeah they were in the street playing. But it just wouldn't enter your head that people would walk into your houses. And they always, they did used to come in and say, you know, have you got a cup of tea or a cup of sugar you can lend me or a drop of milk?

Morris: It was a different community up in Park Terrace I think…There was a girl in school's grandmother used to live there, who my gran knew, and so I remember going to her house a few times at the bottom of Caepistyll Street, but never knew anybody else who lived in Caepistyll Street. Whereas I guess I knew everyone on the Terrace and you know, everyone was very good, and would do anything for anyone there. I remember there were a number of older people that my dad used to go and take firewood to, or give them a ride here, there and everywhere. In fairness, in the years since, people have done it for my mother as well which is very nice. There's still a very good community up there.

Katy: In the summer evenings we would sit on the steps in Winnie's house, opposite your house. And we'd be out there maybe till 12 o'clock at night drinking, laughing and talking having a good chit chat you know, just a neighbourly thing…Well if it was a warm evening you'd go outside and then you'd all mix in together you know, it was just like that. And then on New Year's Eve you know, our front doors would be open and we'd lay on the table a buffet you know and leave a couple of bottles of wine on, or something on the table for them to have a drink, and anybody could go in your house and have a drink or anything. It was safe.

Priest 2: Mr Bill Holley was a highly respected member of St. Joseph's parish who ran the youth club for many years. So much so that the parishioners erected a plague in the hall in appreciation for his youth work. They were a great group but could cause surprises at times. One such event was a trip to Port Eynon beach. When we got there the youngsters off the coach I suddenly realised they had all disappeared. I asked Bill where had they gone? He said 'I don't really know'. They were later found in the Pub called the "The Ship". They were, of course, very happy.

Katy: We could go over Mrs Day's shop with our babies in the shawl and have a little gossip over there and talk about everything that had happened you know.

Mark: You know, we, when we were small, we had a haircut, with Sonia and Nicholas Nazareth's dad! Dowdell's the baker, they were running a chemist as well. All those shops, we knew everybody in all of them. And were in them every day, for something or other.

Sarah: …and I started working, Dowdells, as I said, in the Post Office, and the bakery and they'd come in had a good time. And 10 o'clock she'd come in then, and they'd start talking to each other, ask you what they're going to have tea that night you know… All the little shops…well, well and people, neighbours sometimes, when they'd go down the shop…the Post Office, chemist whatever. That's the only time they would see people sometimes as well. And you did realise that as well and they're standing there, half hour, hour talking to you.

Vince: *(Talking about the role of pubs in the 1970s.)* I think it also put people in contact with one another as in making connections. You know, people probably needed connections for jobs, extra work if they needed anything done on the house or cars. Maybe some people needed a job in a school and they could get fixed up with a job and things like this you know. And thinking of those days, the

67

public sector was much bigger. We had more mines, iron and steel and, of course, more trade with Swansea Docks just 15 minutes' walk down the road. We didn't have the privatisation of Thatcher then. There was a lot of industry. And don't forget trade.

Simon: You know, pubs would have cricket teams and football team. I mean there are no pubs left in the Sandfields. Hardly any pubs left in Greenhill.

Mark: I expect your parents as well, they've grown up in the same community. Very few of them have moved away. There were very few people, I think, living in our community who moved in from the outside. And, you know, I think people had a history there. So, my mother's friends were there. People she'd grown up with, she'd been to school with. Their parents and our grandparents had also grown up together. I think there wasn't some sort of, there wasn't that culture of, which we, I think, embraced subsequently of going to school, moving away, and not going back unfortunately. I think, you know, my mother, she trained as a teacher. She did that in Swansea. I mean, she's lived, apart from a brief period of time when she and my father first got married, she's lived in two houses, I think, her whole life.

Priest 1: And when I arrived, I came round the corner by St Joseph's school and I could see this dark stone, polluted stone effect on the church. I thought it was very depressing, very miserable and I thought 'My God that's the place here...I wouldn't like to be here'. Little did I know that - I was in Ireland then, for my holiday in August - and my sister-in-law sent me a cutting from the South Wales Argos, the Newport paper which said, 'Newport priests first appointment- St Joseph's Swansea'. And that was the first I knew about it.

Priest 2: The first year I was in St. Joseph's we had a Bazaar in the hall. It was well supported it really was a great community event. All the parishioners and non-parishioners took part helping with the stalls and other activities. I was new and hadn't a clue of what was going on. I felt isolated standing in the middle of the hall, so I asked myself 'What do I do with everyone milling around?'. So I concluded the only thing I could do was to smile and say 'hello'. Which worked very well. The parishioners were always very welcoming but one had to push oneself, in other words, make an effort to meet and chat with them. They could be very open about what they thought was wrong, but in general they appreciated the clergy and were always supportive.

Priest 2: The people accepted their clergy very well. I had one experience with the members of the youth club, it taught me a valuable lesson. It was sometime early in 1971 when the New Mass came in. I ask the members would they like to take part in the Mass, perhaps help with the singing? Generally, they seemed amenable but one or two were strongly opposed to the idea and said no. I insisted on them taking part which was a mistake. The members walked out and left me with no club. But later some drifted back and the youth club resumed. I learned a very valuable lesson: one mustn't confront things head on. One has to use the triangular method – in other words there must a way out.

Sarah: *So, do you think you had a lot of power?*

Oh yes, oh definitely.

What power did you have?

Well, the running of the house, the community more or less. The men weren't involved, they went to work, they come home, had their food, up the club. That was my experience yes and I used to do little trips every now and again once a year I used to organise a bus, come and take the women and the children, August Bank Holiday Monday and things like that.

16: Bonds, Bridges and Roads

In his book, *Bowling Alone*, Robert Puttnam, the American sociologist, describes two types of social capital. (37) Bonding social capital builds ties between people within the boundary. It strengthens within, for example, a street, or a social club, or a neighbourhood. It builds deep, mutual support and solidarity between people. The many examples of volunteering and goodwill in previous chapters reflect the strong social bonds in the area at the time.

While they reinforce links within, they don't reach out to bring in people beyond the boundary. Bridging social capital does just that. It builds links to the outside world, spreading messages outside, and bringing outside assets to help inside. And there are examples in Greenhill of bridges being built at this time. For example, visits to Ireland to strengthen the Irish cultural connections; sports and singing events, involving teams, groups and pubs from other parts of Swansea, visiting Greenhill and hosting visits in turn.

A community needs both. Bonds help us get by, and bridges help us get ahead. Too-tight bonds might give us a strong sense of security within, but exclude people from outside. Too few bridges and we fail to notice the weak signals of threats on the horizon.

***

Once more, dereliction created a playground. In 1978, where lower down the Carmarthen Road towards Dyfatty, there'd been a doctor's practice, now emptied, waiting for this and other buildings to be demolished because of the planned widening of Carmarthen Road. At the back of the doctors' practice was a low extension with a lead roof. And, as the latest in a tradition of opportunists, we decided to strip the lead and take it to Shaddicks the scrap dealers, to earn a little paydirt.

Walking to the plunder, with my father's shears hidden in my trousers, I felt liberated and strangely conspicuous. I forgot how to walk. A slow, nonchalant walk? A summer-time, chatty walk? Try to strike the right balance. With shears. Paul, a couple of others, and I arrived looked around, saw no problem, scaled the roof and started to cut. 30 minutes later, we were done. We rolled the lead into tubes then into plastic bags.

But we were inexperienced hustlers, tentative and unconfident. If we take this to Shaddicks, we thought, they'll ask how we got it and we'll have no good answer. The solution, clearly, was to melt it into different shapes. 15 minutes later, armed with matches, a saucepan and a Yorkshire pudding mould tray, we were on our way to the Rockland quarry, and to our favourite hollow, hidden from view by slope and heather. We lit a fire, placed the lead into the pan, and waited. 25 minutes later, we poured the molten metal into the waiting moulds and had around 16 silvery-lead scallops. We looked at each other and knew we could never take these to the men at Shaddicks. Because they were orcs, and they'd look at our dainty, fine lead offerings and laugh. We dumped the pan, the lead and the mould tray, and ended the day as wealthy as we'd started.

***

The A483, Carmarthen Road, is one of the main roads in Swansea, allowing access from the North, through to the city centre via the High Street. After a reorganisation with the city council, the highways department of the county council took on the problem of slow traffic flow on the A483. This wasn't news for those paying attention, and the city council had previously sited road improvement plans at the Guildhall council building. Traffic congestion was the issue. Slow journeys for car drivers created frustrations. And slower journeys meant more noise and emission pollution, adding to concerns for the health of residents alongside the road. And the forecasts for higher traffic flow in the years to come meant that something had to be done.

In the late 1970s, many shops and houses dotted both sides of the road, though mainly on the west side, extending from Dyfatty lights, northwards up to the flat of Zoah bus stop. And the road widening would flatten most of these buildings - at least 182 properties would be demolished along the length of the road, including further north up through Cwmbwrla and on to Fforestfach.

The archives department of Swansea council shows that a public consultation meeting took place on 13th December 1977. (38) Chaired by the chairman of the county highway committee, Cyril Williams, and with the speaker being Mr John, Deputy County highways engineer. The meeting discusses viable routes, including possible by-passes affecting other parts of Swansea. And money, of course: both the cost of alternative solutions and the money available.

Steve Williams, presumably a local resident, is not happy:

> "Mr John has just very effectively dealt with the transport problem on Carmarthen Road, but the people who are here tonight are not only concerned with the transport problem. There is a community problem and an environmental problem…"

The chairman replies:

> "…of course I agree with every word you have said, Mr Williams…the environment and the way people live in communities are extremely important… "

As the meeting progresses, it's clear that a decision has already been made. The consultation is less about listening and more about telling the group what will happen next: a widening of the road, incrementally changing what already exists, bringing quicker and, crucially, affordable results. Later, the Chairman continues:

> "…and we have made the point tonight again and again and again, the scheme we would like to see done with the minimum of voidance *(sic)* of any property and the breaking up of any communities on Carmarthen Road, but I repeat that we just don't have the money to do it."

The South Wales Evening Post reported on the change, concluding:

"It is also a classic case of how the need for improved communications to cope with the traffic explosion and the needs of industrial growth can have a devastating effect on local established communities." (39)

Under increasing pressure, the Chairman, is asked bluntly:

"…it seems to me whatever this meeting decides you are going to do Carmarthen Road. Are you going to do that? All I am asking is yes or no."

Chairman:

"Yes indeed we are going to do Carmarthen Road."

Other:

"Mr Chairman you said, you referred to democracy, I would just like to say you're going ahead with the scheme anyway so what the hell are you doing here."

***

The road widening wasn't all bad news. Dad had a big heart but not for DIY. Our home was often full of part-used materials seeking a purpose: white plastic pipes, washers, a partly torn brown paper bag full of nails. A lonely hammer on a fake wood side surface.

We'd learnt that the hollow, plastic pipes were exceptionally good for firing dried peas long distances. Who was it with me, as we bought a bag of dried peas from Danny Lane's shop, and placed ourselves in the scrub land and the bushes off Waun Wen Terrace, overlooking Carmarthen Road? Anyway, there were two us, hidden in the bushes, each with a 2-foot white plastic pipe, and peas to last the next 30 minutes. We sent them through the air, way over traffic, into the dumping ground of demolished shops on the either side. And then I saw roll up the hill a stumpy, moustachioed man, equal parts Van Morrison and the American golfer, Craig Stadler. Maybe he also moonlighted as an extra in cowboy films. I sent the pea over, lost sight of it, but it struck and clearly stung him. As he rubbed his head and looked around we lay in the dirt and the dust, struggling to contain our laughter. And off he walked, buzzing, up the Carmarthen Road.

We forgot about Mr Van-Stadler for the next two minutes, until a full house-brick thonked the railings in front of us, missing my head by 18 inches. He was all puce, gristle and bristle, clambering over the railings and straining to reach us. We scrambled through the scrub, not knowing how close he was behind. Terror doesn't do facts. I hopped the railings and dropped the 12 or so feet, onto Carmarthen Road in a gap between the traffic, and ran to the other side. The side with the peas.

17: Allan

Our gardens were 60 yards apart. And he's describing growing up in that area, pre and during the second world war, as well as living here in the 1970s. He talks about the role of shops in the area, and how this changed in the late 1970s, as well as his role in the road-widening negotiations. We're in his apartment in a different part of Swansea. He moved here only a few years back, leaving the place he knew so well. Though we haven't seen each other for 40 years, he is typically warm, curious and welcoming.

I was born in Marsden Street, and then they would demolish it to a new area, demolishing the houses. They had to give us somewhere to go, so we were in Griffith John's flat for six months and then moved across to Baptist Well Street. You knew everybody really then. I mean nowadays you don't even know who the next door neighbour is. But yeah, you knew everybody in the whole street.

Even when I lived in Marsden Street, we were the same, it was still close. And I think the possibilities are the war years that made it closer, because with the War years, you would go to the shelters. And there was a shelter in Waun Wen school. So you'd get to know everybody in close, close proximity then. You were practically living together while the air raid was on. And the other shelter, we used to go to was the crypt in the church. Now again, you were all together, you know, so that's why you got close, the War Years brought you close. But that brought all the support closer, and the community sort of grew like that. I mean, you knew people in the next street, you know, as well as your own. It was very close. you'd have a chat and stop to talk.

They did stay in the area. When we moved to Baptist Well Street we were there for 45 years. We didn't really want to move. But then, of course, that's when changes started coming in. The older generation was dying off. You had this situation of builders coming in and buying up the property. Some were let, but others coming in, and you didn't even know them, and that was the thing. I mean some people there now would just walk past you.

One of the things probably, is the fact that everybody was the same. It was all working class. So you had the same mentality, I suppose. It was it was work ethic. And you all had that. This is what it was about. Nearly everybody was working class, when you think about it. But work then, people needed to get work, to, to keep going, I suppose. And that might have been a bit of a time when the closeness might have been losing. Because people were in work. Your mother worked part time, and my wife work part time, with the kids. And so, they weren't there so much, then, as you were previously. We had to get out and work. A lot of women worked in Cwmfelin. My mother worked in Cwmfelin, welding jerry cans, as they called them then, which was just petrol cans. Those were the early days of the 70s. That work ethic always lived with them. So they were there all the time. I mean, even from the fact of putting clothes on the line, you know, they'd put clothes on the line, and they're talking, because the neighbours are putting clothes on the line.

It was tight. And the wages you earned, even then, wasn't high wages. I worked for British Gas - great company to work for - but they never paid big money in the early days. And even when, even in the early 50s money wasn't big. I remember I got to a stage, I think it was nearly four pound a week. I was coming to the last year of my apprenticeship. then I went in the RAF and it went back down. Those are the things you remember. And the money went back down, I thought, Oh God, this is handy. Just got lowered down. OK, you had your food and your uniform but you still was a bit broke.

I can remember, people always looked for a seamstress in those days, because you had to repair things. You, you know, couldn't keep going and buying new, like they do now - throw away, and buy new. And the seamstress those days, was really worth their weight in gold. Because they were looking for things, to repair things. We didn't have the money to buy it.

There were loads of these little shops, and I think that brings you close as well. The corner of Ysgubor Fach Street, Carmarthen Road.

If you come down, with the Red Cow. Now then, there was another little shop, which was house. He was a foreigner. Very, very nice man. Can't remember the name. Because then from there down, between there and Lion street. Yeah, well Strouds was practically right outside there. Now that was a house. The front room, the parlour, if you like. And what happened, in the war years, you had to register with a shop, and give in your identity books, your ration books. That was the main part of the shop. On the corner then of Lion Street you had the Bluebell. Then you had a newsagents in the corner there. Then you go up Lion Street, and you have another little shop on the left. Then you had the outdoor licence, round the corner of Lion Street and Lamb Street.

And you take Carmarthen Road, you had Lanes - It wasn't Aggie's at first, because Aggie used to work at Cwmfelin works as well. But then Danny Lane was there, that was like an ordinary house. And I always remember he used to sell paraffin oil for the lamps. And the paraffin oil was in the corner of the shop, and the bread was over there. Absolutely incredible.

And the next corner there was another shop, a little bit upmarket: Husbands. Of course when you go down then, you had the fish shop and the butchers. Then you had another shop on the other corner. That was like a house. Can't remember his name now. He was a bit of a snob he was, but I can't remember his name. Then you had the fish again, and then the repairing shoes. You'd go down, at the bottom of Symmons Street, there was on Carmarthen Road, a newsagent there. And then you go down, and you had another little shop which became Aggie Lane's. Then of course you had the post office. Then you had another pub, the California. Further down, you had the fish shop. And then as you go by the lights, there was a fruiterers, and everything.

So these different shops really constituted the closeness of everything. But the thing is, this is where they also met people. Because there's so many small shops. They go in every one of them, and they meet people.

What you had, you had, in those days, was a bar. And you had a lounge. So that the lounge is a little bit dearer than the bar because you had, in a bar, your working clothes, if you like. Women could go in the lounge, but in some places, like I remember, the Bluebell having one, the Red Cow, I think most of the pubs - you could go in this little room, just by the front door. A Snug! Yeah, I remember that. I never frequented pubs myself, because I never drank. But knew the places, cos my father used to serve in the Bluebell. The Bluebell, of course, was more upmarket than the Red Cow.

Before the road was widened, they'd emptied the houses and were doing nothing. They didn't knock them down, you know, they just left them. And it wasn't on because they were leaving these houses empty and rats and everything was in them, on Carmarthen Road. We were trying to get things done. And it was a very, very slow process. Alan Williams was the Labour MP. He'd listen. We used to go down regular to the Lyceum. He was very, very good. And it was Williams who got us this meeting with the Highways.

At the time, I, for some unknown reasons, I was chairman of the Waun Wen Action Group. Betty Fry from Colebourne, she was our secretary. Green, the outdoor licence - what's his first name? Damn my memory, because he was, Vice Chairman. Him and his son was on it. We had a few people on it, you know, and we had a young student working for us, as well. We were trying to get the area sorted out. Eventually it came to fruition. You know, after a lot of work, it got double glazing for those people's back gardens that was running onto Carmarthen Road then, with a wider road. Yeah, we did a lot for the community.

18: Teacher 1, Jennifer and Lisa

Teacher 3, Lisa, and Jennifer were involved, directly or indirectly, at St Joseph's school. The teacher was brought into the school from outside the area, with no existing community connections, and is widely acknowledged to be a very effective school leader.. Over time, the teachers and parents stretched the children, taking them on school trips to new places. They developed horizons and ambitions beyond the boundaries of the place-based community. And the school became very successful in the following decades, leading to a demand for places from pupils who didn't live in the area.

Teacher 1: Because it had been on a hill and if you've never been to the school you go in one door and you go down and down and you come out at the bottom of the road. And the playground at that time, which you wouldn't remember it, was like a Black Hole of Calcutta wasn't it?...Basically the wall had never been painted so there was an overhang, sort of, which was open and it was black tar underneath, so it undulated in the sense because it followed the contours of the rain. There was like white on one wall, distemper I would call it going back in those days, with this sort of flaked and everything else. But over-ridingly because of the light situation it appeared dark and dismal. OK on a bright day, but on a damp day...

Lisa: The school did have an excellent reputation. We bought this house and moved here in the December, - started in the January and our neighbours next door but one invited us down and when he said he was going to St Joseph's: 'Oh excellent school, fantastic reputation'

Teacher 1: And that's the thing: reputation is always four or five years behind the actual ability of the level of the school. And that's sometimes for better, sometimes for worse. Because the numbers were running down, and when I used to go to football matches some people say 'Oh I went to St Joseph's' and they would say the school is only concerned with football.

But…I think there was a new change of Priest, and Canon - came and it changed the whole focus in a sense because he could see that…the community basically was becoming too introverted...but in a way it was quite far-sighted for him to realise the dangers…He was brave.

As I said it was a community I think within the community. I don't think people had an awful lot to give their neighbour, but they would share. Because it was a time like when I grew up you wouldn't lock your door, people would come in you know and you had a cup of tea. So you know you'd have a biscuit and a cup of tea and that was the school. We were called the "kit kat school"…Whoever came in, workmen…they got a welcome…In those days when, before we were in control of our budget, I relied on people doing me favours. And it wasn't that I gave them a cup of coffee or anything else to get a favour. But when we needed something they knew we were doing everything possible for the good of the children and they would help us.

The community, I suppose, appreciated that they wanted their children, as you said, to go on and have things that they didn't have, and they would do everything possible for that. So the school was a magnet for them.

But I think the community reflected society. And unfortunately in society in those days you know, the old adage still that the men were the boss of the household. And in fact, if as we said earlier, the women were at home, they didn't have money as such of their own. We had a very strong PTA. It would make about 5 or 6 thousand pounds a year and that was sort of,…20, 25 years ago. Where people helped and enjoyed coming in and so many people probably, on a recollection now, mothers weren't working quite as much…so they had time to come into school.

Jennifer: And the parents would…help out in the nursery…then, and they'd go through the infants and then they're landing in my room. They would accumulate - they were a marvellous group of ladies.

Teacher 1: …then the parents would be meeting each other on the gate - they'd be talking. They were welcome inside the school, you know, to assist and to help. So it gave them status as well. It gave them an involvement with their child's learning because the absorption of watching qualified staff teach their children is the best way …And as the school developed they were the most appreciative of people because they weren't people who had been to university themselves…they wanted education for their children. And when they saw that the school was trying to achieve that then they gave you a 110%.

Lisa: I would say that the women were the workers in school. In the school community we didn't see the dads. They were working.

Jennifer: Only if there were painting jobs to be done on a weekend or helping.

Lisa: And we were in the days of no-checks. There was no security in the school in those days, until Dunblane, free access into a school. You know you can't go into schools now unless you have a CRB check but in those days the door was open.

Jennifer: I'd be sitting there lunch time, never left. Door knock…'yeah what's the matter?', 'Can you ask Mr - if he wants a game of football?' And I'd knock his door, he'd have his roll in his hand. I said 'Sir the boys want to know do you want a game of football?' He'd take his roll, and go out and play football at dinner time, every day.

Teacher 1: No, it wasn't that I played football with the children. If you remember the school reached the stage there were 430, 440 juniors…it declined to something like 220 at one stage and then it'd grew to 440 odd junior children but the playgrounds were very small. And…because the boys loved football, the community loved football and everything else. What they would do which is common: the best five footballers would pick themselves right. So the best five footballers would be in one team and then all, with a couple of others, and then the rest would play. Now when they were playing if the ball jammed or something they'd pick the ball up and say 'touch', right? Now the other children couldn't compete against these, these were their role models and the leaders as such. And so it was arguments and pushing and shoving and people used to get hurt because they'd kick the ball across the yard, which people you know didn't want to be involved in football. So it was much easier to go up there and control that football and make sure that it was reasonable, rather than do anything else. Because otherwise my problems were far greater in the lunch time.

If you liked children and if you are able to communicate them - you know, you had to say 'Rob' or whatever. And with that involvement then, and of course as discipline got so much better and staff were very much together on it, my role got so much easier. In fact my role as a disciplinarian was almost non-existent. My role was the friend of the children and that made a difference... But the community, as I said, it was the basic community respected you, they respected you as a teacher... You were important in their eyes by the very nature of being a teacher. ... I wasn't their friend, but I was a friendly to them.

Lisa: Theresa was in Year 6 Leaving and she always said 'when Mr - came it was as if the film in the camera changed from black and white to colour.

Jennifer: And I said 'It's like this: you've got children in this school from all walks of life, we've got solicitors' children, doctors' children, gypsies, the roma.' I said 'and from the outside estates of Townhill, Blaenymaes…being bussed in because the parents want their children to have something.' And I said 'once they walk through that door those children are treated all the same. They're equal. Every child is equal here regardless.'

Lisa: When we came to the time when school was data-driven, and…St Joseph's was passed a socially deprived area because where there so many free meals…but, I think if we think about what is socially deprived, those children were not deprived. We had extra funding for cleaning the teeth. The children's teeth were so bad in school that we had medical staff came in. And towards the end every child had a toothbrush in St Joseph's, given to them free. And the children had to have their teeth cleaned after dinner to try and

82

overcome the teeth decay in the school. Because their diet was wrong at home. Financially, they were deprived because the incomes weren't going into those houses, but I think every one of the children at St Joseph's was loved. At home and in school.

Jennifer: He was the head inspector. And I think it was him who wrote in that report... 'When you enter the doors of St Joseph's, it's as if you're walking into Aladdin's cave, of the good things that were there for children'... I think it was just people were happy and secure. And that's the important thing I think the children need. They got the boundaries, they knew where they were, they were happy within, they were treated fairly and there was laughter.

19: Looking out: 1976-1982

On weekday nights, before leaving for the social club, Dad would sit down and watch the nine o'clock news with the same rapt attention as he gave the horseracing on a Saturday afternoon. Both were a routine and welcome distraction from work worries. It was still a battlefield, according to the front pages of the Swansea Evening post. If not quite the carnage of the early 1970s, when more than 14 million annual strike days occurred on average in the UK, it was still bubbling.[d] (40)

The dustmen were on strike, as were 300 craft workers at BP Llandarcy, who supported 2 suspended fellow workers, and 2,000 Ford workers at Jersey Marine. TV repairers too - on 15th May 1978, 500 sets were waiting for repair in Swansea alone. (41) In January 1979, the local newspaper reported that the Transport and General Workers' Union (TGWU) was likely to make official the strike of the 35K lorry drivers, affecting fuel, fresh food, and likely to affect the rail network too. The pressure was building, and 2-3 million workers may be off work within two weeks.

Anthony Hopkins left the UK for Los Angeles in September 1977, complaining: the attitude in Britain is one of grudge and constant moaning. Everyone seems so humourless. (42)

British Leyland was a lodestone of industrial action. With 30,000 jobs in the UK, and 1,000 at the Felinfoel plant, near Swansea, it was regularly in the news. At their biggest plant in Longbridge, Birmingham, 18,000 workers voted within minutes for strike action,

---

[d] The average strike days per year in the UK was nearly 4 million between 1965-69; just over 14 million between 1970-74; more than 11.5 million between 1975-79; and just under 10.5 million between 1980 - 1984. The yearly average through the 1990s was around 824,000.

on hearing that Derek Robinson ("Red Robbo") had been sacked from his role as chairman of shop stewards, for publishing a 16-page booklet, urging workers to resist the executives' streamlining plan.

All this took a toll in the 1978-79 Winter of Discontent. Inflation was round 10%, the government had been asking for wage restraint, but wasn't getting it from a workforce worried about having a job, and whose incomes had lost value.

And when the Labour Prime Minister, Jim Callaghan, returned to the UK from an economic world summit in the Caribbean on 10th January 1979, he said: "I don't think other people in the world would share the view [that] there is mounting chaos." (43). Margaret Thatcher replaced him as Prime Minister on May 4th, 1979. Her start was economically dire. In early March 1980, the government was studying five reports for prospects for the British economy: falling output and profits, higher inflation and unemployment. One report from the London Business School brought no cheer:

"The prospects are that the next four years will be considerably worse than the last four." (44)

In 1981, more than 25% of property renters in Swansea were behind on their payments. (45) When I left for university In September 1982, the unemployment rate in Wales was at 17.4% - around 1 in 6 people. (46) School leavers were struggling to find work. The Welsh office was looking at significant investment into the city they hoped would result in new jobs in hotels, a redevelopment of the maritime quarter, construction, high technology, knowledge-based small businesses, as well a seafront residential development.

***

While new sources of economic growth were sought, and heroic efforts launched to reclaim the Lower Swansea Valley, bacterial levels in the city's main bay were tested in 1981, for the first time since 1973. If urgency had previously been lacking, the test results now provided it. The council accepted that raw sewage, toilet paper and contraceptive sheaths had washed up on the beach. Average coliform levels had increased at several beach sites and were above their 1973 levels, and at twice the level advised by the World Health Authority. All of which resulted in £20 million being promised for further investment to sort the problem, to be spearheaded by the city's Labour MP, Alan Williams.

Worry adores a ready target, and while money anxieties grew, threats from the world outside were plentiful. A whooping cough epidemic was predicted for Wales in December 1977. And in August 1978, an awful smallpox leak at Birmingham medical schooled led to Janet Parker, a medical photographer, contracting a disease which was thought to have been eliminated globally a year earlier. There was widespread fear, and steps taken to source contacts and vaccinate those potentially affected in the UK's second largest city. By the end of the outbreak, 1982 contacts at the hospital had been vaccinated. Parker died from the disease, and the events also led to the death of Henry Bedson, the head of the department of medical microbiology. In 1979, the papers also predicted that Red Flu would affect our schoolkids. Believed extinct, it had reappeared in China and would now visit us. (47) And in 1981 there was a case of malaria at Singleton Hospital.

Roland Clements was the head of the University's careers advisory service. And in 1980, he said that Swansea was losing some of its best brains because local employers are not active enough in offering jobs to those recently graduated. He dismissed the argument that this would take jobs from locals: new jobs and organisations would be created through having more talented people create more competitive businesses. (48)

In the late 1970s and early 1980s, Swansea City football team was climbing the divisions, all the way to first in 1981. For some reason, welcoming outsiders was no problem here. In this period, manager John Toshack used his Liverpool connections to introduce, among others, Tommy Smith, Ian Callaghan, Emlyn Hughes, Phil Boersma, Alan Waddle and Ray Kennedy. Swansea's climb galvanised the city and they surprised everyone by leading the first division in 1982, with only 6 games to go. The unbearable tension was resolved with floppy performances, and the team finished 6th.

That was the world out-there, mediated through television and newspapers. More personally, these were the teenage years, and strange things were happening to the minds and bodies of me and my friends. I'm sitting in Mr Eustis' English class at Bishop Vaughan school. Bored, again. On the blackboard, he's drawing the tree structure of an essay: 'You start with a main theme, then branch off to 3 or 4 small themes, then add some details under each…' I'm daydreaming while feigning enough attention, (not imagining how many times teachers have seen this). I see the image on the blackboard, but also have the odd sense that the image is, right now, imprinting on my brain. It's a nibbling-feeling of neuronal change.

Chris played music through the window of his parlour. And we sat: Jonathan, Paul, Ed, Carl, me, listening to John Martyn sing about Solid Air. Drab Sundays, with the late-afternoon stomach churning, might be saved by visits to Cousin Terry and his music collection. Piledriver by Status Quo - the aural equivalent of being hit by a housebrick. (I didn't know then that this was the same address where my mother had gone to recover after the stillbirth.)

When Terry Griffiths won the world snooker championship in 1979, it brought closer to home the mysterious world of TV celebrities. He bought his suits where Mam worked: "Terry! Lovely man".

We moved from Symmons Street in 1979, with some kicking and screaming. We needed more space, said Dad, and he was right. Our new house on Carmarthen Road had enough of that, but we'd left our place in a collective, and our new home was a soulless, social vacuum, on a raised terrace overlooking the A483 dual carriageway.

***

In the late 1970s and early 1980s, teenage years were mainly about not getting what I wanted, and uniting with the injustices of the world. I identified with the talented, the marginalised, and, ideally, the

87

misunderstood ones. Why be half-hearted?

It's June 1978, with the radio playing in our over-heated car. David Gower is about to face his first ball in international test cricket, against Pakistan at Edgbaston. I'm excited for Gower - he seems to have the gift. He's all about grace, timing and redirecting the red ball. A featherer and a channeler of energy. But I've seen talent bludgeoned by force before. No worry - he pulls his first ball for four runs. "Oh, what a princely entry", says John Arlott.

John McEnroe arrived on my television in 1979, beating Jimmy Connors in the semis, then Bjorn Borg in the final of the WCT in Dallas. He wasn't Borg, and he wasn't mainstream. He might change a few things. And he could do jaw-dropping things with his imagination and a tennis racquet. And he fought on a narrow ledge, where his fury at authority might sabotage his talent. It was painful, compelling viewing, and Dad used to enjoy my agonies as I watched McEnroe's struggles with the whole universe. In the fight between you and the world, back the world, said Kafka, but I didn't know him, and I was too wrapped up in McEnroe's. And when Borg beat McEnroe in the 1980 final, after THAT tiebreak, it was a reminder of pragmatism's strengths. It was Netherlands versus West Germany all over again. But it was also redemption, as McEnroe, in defeat, was welcomed by the crowd. Something had changed. And when he won Wimbledon in 1981, the forming was complete.

All of these patterns were swirling around. The excitement of music and sport, and people from faraway places contrasted with the mundanity of everyday school life. And, fair to say, I wasn't one of life's thunderers. I was a dreamer and a procrastinator. It took me time to know what I thought about things, and most of that happened inside my head. Absent-mindedly, I'd strip away old layers of wallpaper in our lounge, and, coming back to awareness, find myself nibbling the dusty, flaking, decades-old fibres. I had a flexible relationship with time, rarely being in a rush, but often anxious about being ambushed by my own forgetfulness and missing something important. A deep well of incompetence and no rush to act meant little got done.

A high point of my day's end would be to lay on the sofa with a glass of milk and 4 chocolate digestives, purring inwardly to acknowledge my due reward after an exacting day. My father was worried – what would happen to this bundle of strangeness...?

Dad was soft, sentimental and tender at a time when these things weren't discussed. He was also a wonderful singer. He sang Sinatra and Dean Martin, Johnny Cash, Neil Diamond and more. And he told me of the time when he knew he'd snared my mother with a song, when they were young and in their blueberry pomp.

He was also edgy and unsettled, his nails always bitten, often on the move, propelled more by his internal nervous configuration than the demands of the situation. On our summer holidays to Devon, Cornwall, Sussex or Kent, he'd drive my mother crazy by soon wanting to leave wherever we'd just arrived. No wonder he'd enjoyed being a lorry driver in his younger years – he could take off and move whenever he wanted.

He was thin-skinned and easily hurt, and he could be prickly. He'd fight back, usually with words, though he also told me that part of being a man was to be ready to fight, if that was needed. But I never saw him hit anyone, including us, though we gave plenty of opportunities. He was intuitive, very judgemental about people, and usually right. "Give him the wide berth. He's a bladder", he said about a friend of mine. He'd seen people take the wrong path, and he was anxious about my own.

Given the prevailing code of silence on emotions, he couldn't possibly say: "I'm worried about you – how are you going to earn a living?" Instead, he expressed concern in sniping comments, which rankled with me, because I knew there was a grain of truth in them:

"Robert, you're lazy. There's no shape on you," he'd say, despairing. "Oh...get stuffed..." I'd blurt, and walk out the room, again.

I saw the Stranglers live in Cardiff in October 1979, and sat at the back, safely away from the mayhem nearer the stage. The Sex Pistols sang about Bodies, and loosened screws I didn't know I had. As I thrashed my air guitar in the front room of our home, lost in thrall, I suddenly knew he was there. And the slow turn to the window confirmed it. Dad never knew I had this energy. Neither did I. And I had nowhere to put it. Life was revealing itself through a dark veil. And his words came from a different time, and a different set of expectations of what was good and bad. And the words stung - criticism from a parent always hurts. Maybe there was something wrong with me…

Stuck together, the game continued. And, seeing his growing despair with my inaction, I understood this as a source of my power. I revelled in shrugging my shoulders and expressing a general vagueness. I opposed his suggestions that I become Head of Apples at the local wholesaler. I'd raise my eyebrows (and less than half a lip) to convey disgust. His eyebrows twitched to show impatience and frustration.

We became pale parodies of ourselves, and our relationship one of increasingly bitter and entrenched opposition. The lightness of our earlier years had gone. He touched my sores and wounds, pointed out my inadequacies, and while I loved him, I sometimes hated him at this point.

And then he'd surprise me. In 1982, Betty Richards, our school headteacher, announced a visit to Russia: 4 days in Leningrad and 4 in Moscow. Cost: £180. I didn't think we could afford it, but something about it excited me, and I asked Dad if I could go. "Of course" he said, with barely a heartbeat. I was stunned. And in February of that year, I was in solidly communist Russia with a 6th form school group on an unforgettable trip.

***

By now I'd learnt to harness my attention for schoolwork. No-one in our family had been to university and I saw the exams as the gateway to something different. At 6th form in Bishop Vaughan school, there'd be talk about what to do next, which universities to apply to and why.

The flutter of possibilities. Back home, and in the streets where I lived, there was rarely talk of ambition and development. The more my leaving became imminent, the more it felt like a toxic secret and a stone on my chest. Was I wrong to want something else? Was I being disloyal to people I'd known forever?

Strong bonds in a place can have their dark side. They can exclude people as much as include. They may limit advancement and leave an area insular and disconnected, unless there are also strong bridges beyond the community boundary. At their worst, they might be oppressive and conformist, and restrict ways out of poverty and exclusion. (49) Some of these intuitions visited my mind at this time. As did the prospect of change and excitement. And the simple truth that going to university was a way of avoiding work. All this caused a rumbling domestic tension, and I wanted it to end.

And in the summer of 1982, I got the 'A' level results I needed. I was off. But suddenly, leaving was compromised, and I blame the people at Dunlop Sports marketing department. They'd released the McEnroe Maxply tennis racquet, replacing the earlier Maxply Fort - a gorgeous racquet with touch and response. McEnroe was using the new racquet and look at him. By now he was the world's best player. I had to have one, but couldn't afford it. So I stole one from a sports shop.

A few days later, there was a firm knock at the front door. I opened it and found a big, broad policeman looking steadily at me:

"Robert?"

"Yes…"

"Have you bought a tennis racquet in the last week?"

"Er, yes."

"Can I see it please?"

Thanks to the ineluctable forces of capitalism, my parents were at work. He stood outside, while I walked upstairs to my bedroom, brain-numb, thinking gone. I brought it down and handed it over. He

91

held it in his hands, checked the brand, perhaps registering a mild disappointment with my choice of racquet. He handed it back to me, holding my gaze and said, slowly: "I'm going to deal with some other things for the moment. If I don't come back within the week, consider yourself lucky."

It was a long week, and I wondered whether, after everything, I may not be off to university. But he never came back. I think he probably thought: 'This idiot did something impulsive and stupid. But he's not a career criminal.' He knew I'd done it, I knew he knew, and he knew I knew he knew. He'd made his point.

I learnt something about me and recklessness and resolved not to be a child of impulse. And I learnt a little about marketing. The Maxply McEnroe was crap. A sorry piece of wood, with no joy. All smoke and mirrors, McEnroe's name and a higher price.

A few weeks later, Uncle Bernard drove me, Mam and Dad to Portchester on the South Coast. It was a long and quiet drive, and I remember very little about it. He dropped me off at Viv and Dave's house, and we unloaded and said a quick and awkward goodbye. Years later, Bernard told me that my mother cried all the way home.

A few days later, I started my business degree with a work placement at Cyanamid in Gosport. And, in those first few weeks, I ordered a pint at a local pub. A man with a vibrant, ginger moustache stood beside me, 13 feet tall and made of oak. He looked at me and said simply: "In this country, we speak English".

***

In the summer of 1986, I returned home after the degree. In my old bedroom that summer, everything seemed smaller and detached. I felt rootless, changed and more than a bit lost. I saw an ad in some national paper, rang them and landed a job in London, selling advertising space to kitchen manufacturers. It wasn't a skill I possessed, and the job lasted until lunchtime on the first day. Nonetheless, I'd made the move, and the momentum felt good.

John Beale was the Director of Education at West Glamorgan

council. And in August 1987, he said yes to my application for a grant for tuition fees for a Masters' course in London. This time, I really was gone.

20: So what? The value of community

Evidently, this neighbourhood of Greenhill had been a tight and cohesive one for around 100 years. From the earlier years of scrambling for acceptance and legitimacy; through the decades of relative stability, when the church, school and social club institutions were formed; the neighbourhood slowly developing shops, pubs and other places for people to gather. All of which consolidated the social and cultural identity of the place. Then the more recent decades of housing clearances, rupturing relationships, followed by attempts to re-stabilise then a challenge to cohesion again, as road widening removed meeting places.

What was the value of community cohesion up to this point? What did it matter?

For many in the area there was a sense of mutual support. That might be practical support, where neighbours fed children whose parents were working late that evening. Or took friends' children on summer trips for the day, as did my mother, and many others. These things were common.

There was emotional support. Many neighbours were there for each other in difficult times. That might mean being present when people were worrying about work and income, or relationship difficulties, or the everyday stuff of life.

There'd also have been a degree of financial support. Some shops would have given credit – "Pay me on Friday, after Thursday's pay packet". People knew, trusted and relied upon each other – there was a high degree of interdependence, borne out of economic necessity. And the circulation of money would have provided another type of financial support. £5 spent locally would have remained in the area for some time, as it circulated from customer to shop owner, to other local shops, to the pub, and back into the home. Without any grand design, money spent stayed local and benefitted local people.

The area also felt safe and the perception of crime was low. Neighbours watched out for unsociable acts, and told parents when their darling child had crossed the neighbourly line. This intricate web of people-knowing-people acted as a collective and internalised means of social control. A point reinforced by Jane Jacobs, the chronicler of thriving city life:

> "The first thing to understand is that the public peace — the sidewalk and street peace — of cities is not kept primarily by the police, necessary as police are. It is kept primarily by an intricate almost unconscious network of voluntary controls and standards among the people themselves, and enforced by the people themselves." (50)

And the area was welcoming, certainly to people who lived there. There was a warmth, and a friendliness which was characteristic of the people and place and time. There were many examples of volunteering in the area. All of this made living there a better experience. Over time, Welsh and Irish had integrated effectively, making the area distinctive for its customs, and where people felt a degree of pride for being part of something distinctive, bigger than themselves and with a heritage worth preserving.

Breaking it down like this doesn't reflect what it was like. It was just living. And much of our time was spent there and not elsewhere. It gave a safe space for exploration, play and excitement in my younger years, and a place to grow bored and restless in my later teens. As Raymond Williams the Welsh writer said, culture is ordinary. (51) And this way of living in this place, with its long history, (of which I was mainly unaware), well…it was just how we lived.

When the Carmarthen Road was widened, and shops and residences removed, it ended thousands of conversations that would have taken place every single day. While the formal institutions – church, school and social club – were the official places of ceremony and meeting, these neighbourhood places also contributed hugely to the social cohesion. These were the places where informal talk happened, gossip was shared, transactions done, money was given, taken, or put on credit; friends and acquaintances met by chance, and by arrangement. This swirl of enjoyable social activity strengthened the bonds that led to people seeing and helping each other, which fed more of the same. And this pattern – hidden in plain sight - was the source that fortified the place for over 100 years.

In the late 1970s, supermarkets were arriving in the area, in Cwmbwrla to the north, and High Street to the south. People could buy everything in one visit to one place. It had an economic and a convenience logic. And, perhaps, for some small shop owners and staff, the road widening might have been a relief. Time for something different…

The road was widened because traffic flow, air pollution, and money mattered more than protecting the system of the Greenhill community. It's relatively simple to count cars, noxious emissions and pounds, and payoffs to home and shop owners. It's much harder to calculate the value of the relationship ties that benefit people through safety, well-being, financial, practical and emotional support. Also, cars, buildings and money can be seen in the short-term, whereas the value of the community was dispersed, often private, and hidden from outsiders. And, perhaps, as this became a habitual part of everyday life, it also became taken-for-granted by the locals.

Later, the effect of the road widening would become clearer to locals:

> "I do remember some years ago, a once-government minister that retired. I arranged for her to meet some of the female residents of the area, and she was promising them: 'Well we can do this, and we can talk about doing that…' And one of the ladies said to her, 'Well yes, but we've heard all this before. You often come up here promising things and you never do anything. The only thing you've ever given us is driven a 4-lane highway through the middle of the community." (Simon)

The road widening marked the end of a period of community re-stabilising. When the shops and pubs disappeared, the physical effect was immediate, but the social changes took longer. There were still long memories in the minds of many residents, and a deep reservoir of goodwill between people. But the everyday nourishing of the cycle that strengthened social bonds had disappeared, and these bonds began to weaken.

21: Pieces: leaving and returning

Whenever I tried to explain what it was like growing up in this part of Swansea to people, especially to my southern-english friends, they didn't get it. The looked at me blankly. I felt like a cloying, clinging creature, trying to wring the gist of meaning of a culture and a way of life I'd already rejected. It was difficult to make sense of it to myself. And so, for a long time, I forget about it.

For a long time, the UK economy had been slowly shifting economic value and jobs from manufacturing to services. Even back in 1881, there were more jobs in services than manufacturing. This accelerated through the mid-twentieth century, and by 2011, 81.1% of UK jobs were service-based, with only 8.9% in manufacturing. (52)

In 1982, the term 'knowledge economy' was appearing. It meant work where ideas and mental productivity mattered, because these may lead to new brands, patents, products, services, technologies. This was work I could imagine myself doing. (By 2019, 39% of UK businesses were 'knowledge-intensive'.) (53) I absorbed myself in the work of the knowledge economy, and got paid for developing ways for people to learn about leadership and creativity and innovation. I became more interested and ambitious about work. And I got better at doing it, and identified with people doing work like mine. I lectured, trained and consulted and joined the middle class. Work took me to live in London and Bristol, and to assignments in Chicago, Bengaluru, Beijing, Sao Paulo, Stockholm, Helsinki, Florence, Munich and Budapest.

I met my wife at work. And I met people who became life-long friends and associates in that way that interesting work in privileged spaces can bring. As I scrabbled for footholds in this unfamiliar not-home, I gradually became a version of me that I recognised. Through my twenties and early thirties, I was a regular-enough visitor to Swansea. It still held me tight and welcomed me. Though, in those years, I would often feel tense as I neared the city. And, deeper, I still felt I'd been disloyal, though no-one said this. Vindication at becoming and unease at leaving. A sense of cleaving.

***

98

Taylor: I mean I ended up in a job that I'd never heard of when we were at school. I didn't know the sort of job existed and they probably even didn't. And I used to look around at the sorts of people, the work that they did, and the only people I knew either worked in an office or factory or they were a teacher and that was it. And I knew I didn't want to do any of those things, although I did end up in an office, so I was very happy to go away. I always used to go back with my mother there, but I never felt any inkling whatsoever to go back there...I mean I will go back because I'm still friendly with some people, but it never entered my head the moment I left that I'd end up back there.

Mark: I felt excited, I think. When I left, Rob, I think I expected to go back, you know, I didn't expect to leave and not to go back to live there. And I never really made a conscious decision not to return there. But you know, things happen don't they? You know, you meet people, job opportunities, come up that sort of thing. And before you know it, you haven't gone back. I mean, the other thing about it, I think was that you know, I was part of a friendships' group at school, I expect you as well. Where many of us, I don't know 10-12 of us perhaps, all went away to a university...I think all the boys I went away to university with, I don't think any of them went back to Swansea to live...In some ways, you know, in terms of industry, South Wales was closing down. And it was a big time of them, you know, political and industrial upheaval. I mean, that's not what kept me away. There are always jobs for doctors, I suppose. But yeah, you know, I think people have opportunity, their expectations changed. And yeah, I mean, my mother, worrying that when I went away, I wouldn't go back... I know I thought she was worrying about nothing. But of course, she was right.

Vince: I think I did miss being there. Being with the family, with the community, just being what it was to be living in that part of Swansea. Rather than coming back to Swansea and living somewhere else, Gorseinon, Blaenymaes, wherever. That's where we were sort of born and raised... I wanted to come back to it, just to be home there and I think I enjoyed life more there.

Taylor: I was delighted. I said to you, as a kid when I was growing up, when I was getting older as a teenager, I always thought I would leave, I always thought I would go to university. I mean my mother was not pushy as a parent, although she was a teacher in education, I never thought for one moment that I wouldn't go to university. I know it took me a few attempts to pass my A levels to get there. After that I never ever thought I'd go back and so I just, I was perfectly happy really. I had a bit of a moment on the day you go off. I never thought for a second I'd go back to live there…and I never have gone back to live there. I think, and it sounds awful to say it, I mean I've still got friends in Swansea, but I always think 'oh it seems a bit of a lack of imagination to stay there' and it's the wrong thing to say. You can have a perfectly happy life, but for me, if I'd ended up there, and it's not anything about the community, but it would have been a real failure not to come out of there. That was more about Swansea I think than it was about Greenhill. I never really felt that I'd find a life I wanted to live there. I don't know why. Partly because I thought I knew I was going to be gay and I couldn't imagine being gay in Swansea.

Mark: I'm very, very fond of it. It always looks a mess. I think physically, I mean, that never changes. That sort of fantastically uninspiring drive into town, off the M4, past Jersey Marine and all that. But I love going back there.

Peter: This is what we did, or this is what I do, then that's what job you should be in. You went to university: 'Oh brilliant, you've gone to university' which means you've got a proper job: 'Oh he's upper class now - he's been to university'. There's still that type of thing because that's the way it was…. I remember - I'd gone to university: 'Oh my god, look out, Professor Peanut's back.' As if, there we are then, I've been and bettered myself, damn for me.

Vince: I felt you know you met people more, you know your neighbours more, you rubbed shoulders with people more. I didn't do that in London, and I think it was impossible - you didn't get to know your next door neighbours. The only big shopping centre was the Ilford Exchange and again I had to drive to the shopping centre. To me in Swansea, just on the doorstep, you just walked down…and you've got a quality of shop you know, and I thought Swansea was better…it was the sea and all the rest of it, the beach and I just thought just being at home was better. For me anyway.

Mark: I'd been in London for a while. And I was at home, (in Swansea), having one of those conversations on a Sunday morning, outside our house, you know, on the doorstep type of thing. And - came down the hill…he was on his way to the club on a Sunday lunchtime…He said hello to me, and he walked halfway down the hill, you know, towards where we'd have gone into school. And he stopped. And he came all the way back up the hill. I don't know who I was talking to outside the house. So he said to me, 'Mark, I meant to tell you: our –'s gone to London, keep an eye out for him.'

22: Mam's end

Mam's cough is getting worse, Paula's letter said. From the mid 1980s onwards, Mam's health began to suffer. She'd been a smoker until her mid-50s, and in a family where emphysema had killed two of her siblings.

The doctors diagnosed emphysema or asthma, or some combination of the two. And from 1986, her breathing was aided by the inhaler, ventolin. She was given steroids, which gave her some relief but also made her skin translucent. Through the late 1980s and 1990s, her medical record is a slew of efforts to mitigate the disease. Incomprehensible terms, scrawled on rough pages. "SOB" – 'shortness of breath' appears increasingly regularly.

It was a time of reckoning. In the early 1990s, she divorced my father. They'd been growing apart for a long time, and the tensions had become harder to ignore. She tried to move out of the old family home, the months passed and she lost a lot of weight. She developed depression and was prescribed Prozac, which helped. Within a few months she'd found another place and was living alone.

21/7/97: Dr –B's records show that in November 1996, Mam's lung capacity was at 47%. It'll be less now. She has sudden small gasps of breath. I pretend not to hear them. Dr H- says there are a few years left in her. There's a 5-year waiting list for a lung transplant. "Best to stay with the lungs God gave her."

Hospital visits became more common. At the start, these were raw, rebounding times of fear and hope, and learning to read between the lines of medics' comments. In June 1997, I visited her in hospital during a first serious episode.

June 97: She looks blotchy, wasted, all plugged in with tubes, afraid and scared. Her mind is still as sharp as ever. It's heart-breaking to see her like this. This woman I love so much, whose eyes lit up and who mouthed 'Robert', as I walked through the room. Her breathing is an orchestra. Wheezes and rattles in rhythm.

28/7/97: Mam due out of hospital tomorrow. She ate a whole chicken leg today. It's a relief that she recovered from a second chest infection last week. I have learnt to doubt all positive signs. How can we get her to eat more?

In 1998, after one of these increasingly regular hospital stays, she contracts the superbug, MRSA. And then gets the Diff C toxin. She survives it all, though it leaves a mark. *Her food intake is pitifully low,* says a consultant. She would eat like a bird, picking at morsels, chewing and swallowing with difficulty.

The combination of reduced lung capacity, less walking, less calorie intake, illness and the worry from it all, mean she is often exhausted. But she had a ton of willpower. My daughter, Ella, her first grandchild, was born in early 2001, and she somehow held Ella on her lap.

I was staying with her in the summer of that year. Just the two of us would be there, and I had decided to ask how she felt about death. In case she wanted to talk about it but was holding back because she didn't want to upset me. I didn't like the idea of her privately having to deal with the unsaids, worrying about us, as well as her other burdens.

"I'm not afraid of dying. I'll be with Vera and Mam. I just don't want to die alone." (Her sister, Vera, had died a couple of years back, along with her mother, Sarah-Ann, in 1979.)

By late 2001, she was *"Requesting vitamin drinks. Any flavour, except peach."* And had an oxygen cannister in her home, to help the breathing. And in January 2002, she was in hospital again, at Singleton. We all visited, and the family communication channels clicked into their usual, efficient action.

She'd had a lot of care and medical attention in the difficult years leading up to this. Her GP had been very assiduous. Consultants and homecare had done what they could to aid the suffering from emphysema, a wasting disease than can be treated but not cured.

The nurses on the ward were a gas. One of them used to joke with Mam, offering to hang her on a peg, out of the 4th floor window, to dry her after her morning wash. And now Mam was talking about being home again. Almost making plans. And we were complicit, smiling and encouraging her, while wondering about the odds.

I asked for a talk with a doctor. "The difficult thing is", I hesitated, "that she's been in and out of hospital so many times… We don't know whether to hope."

"Well, she won't be coming out this time. She's coming to the end of her time now." said Doctor C-. "There's no point in taking more tests. We know what's wrong with her. All we can do is make her more comfortable."

It wasn't as brutal as that may sound. He was responding to what I'd asked and watching me carefully as he spoke. By his side was an assistant, a more junior doctor, who said nothing, but she noted my silence and the moistening eyes. When they'd left, I imagined them talking about what had happened, and that such conversations do happen and are necessary.

Things changed in the final week. The pieces coalesced and brought clarity. Tiredness grabbed her, the delirium started and she'd drift in and out of sleep. One time she woke up suddenly and said:

"Was I talking about curtains then? I dreamt I was taking them up…"

And another time, springing upright in her bed, straight from sleep:

"I'm not dead yet, you know."

"Unbelievable", said Sheila to Pat, the remaining sisters sitting with her.

And one day a song might have visited her, because she awoke and asked Paula to play *Sinner or Saint* by Sarah Vaughan. Something that meant a lot to her as a young woman.

In that week, I agonised about taking a 2-day work assignment near Reading. I told my new boss what was going on back in Swansea. I took the job, with the proviso that he'd be ready to replace me, in case I had to leave suddenly. On the Thursday night, the call came from my sister:

"Mam's taken a turn for the worse. The staff are recommending you get back as soon as possible."

I drove up the M4 through the appalling evening rain on the Thursday 31st January 2002. Probably affected by the visibility, a lorry didn't see me, and pulled out into the middle lane, missing me by a foot or two. It was the day after Ella's 1st birthday.

When Mam died at dawn on Saturday 2nd February 2002, she weighed 3.5 stone. Within an hour, members of the family stood in the ward's lounge area, looking wretched and not knowing what to say. But the ward matron knew exactly what to say: "You'll miss her. She was a strong woman and you'll miss her."

An hour or so later, I went into her room to collect some items. Her body lay on the bed to my right, and I couldn't resist. I glanced at her and saw what was left. Her skin was a grey-green mask, and I knew for certain that what had been my mother wasn't in that body.

She died at 70. I was 38, too young to deal with it, and too busy to stop. The following months were a blur.

18/6/02: Feeling drained and heavy around the eyes. Stomach is churning and sometimes paining. Diarrhoea - fairly mild – IBS? Is it the anxiety that's emptying me inside out? I think my dreams are fucked up too. Last night I dreamt that England beat Brazil 7-6. A poodle sat on the ball on 88 mins, and the ref blew up for full-time.

16/01/03: Yes I do feel burdened, weighed down, heavy with my history. I'd like to feel free lighter, free of the unspecifiables, the drag downs. I'm wondering if I'm mildly depressed or just the same as everyone else."

Getting out of bed was harder. There was a weight on my shoulders, and I couldn't be bothered with much. This was something different to the winter effect, and I went to the GP, who asked me some questions, told me I may have a mild depression and gave me the names of 3 counsellors. I chose Jan.

The weeks and the sessions that followed were lively and helpful. She was insightful, empathetic and challenging. We talked about the fear of getting angry, the fear of rejection, damaged and damaging relationships, of self-control and the cost of self-control. And as weeks and months past, I felt the welcome return of myself. Something lifted and I began to feel lighter and more interested in the world.

Part 3: Reforming

23: The Social infrastructure

"People die twice, first socially, then clinically. We need to do more about the first." (54)

40 years have passed since those days of leaving Greenhill. And the institutions of the area have had plenty of change. The church became Swansea's only cathedral in 1987, ninety nine years after its opening. While its institutional status is confirmed, it has had to contend with serving an ageing population, while general interest in religion has declined. The church community groups that brought people together have also largely disappeared.[e] The primary school is thriving, with outstanding results, and attracting many applications from wider parts of Swansea, and from a much more ethnically diverse population. But the social club struggled with ever-diminishing attendances. Younger people didn't want to go there. After generations of music, drinking and socialising, it closed in 2014.

And in the informal spaces of the neighbourhood itself, the shops, pubs, homes and gathering places have not been replaced on the Carmarthen Road. Where people used to stop, buy, sell, talk, drink, laugh, argue, gossip and wonder, now people largely move on through, to elsewhere.

In 'Palaces for the People', Eric Klinenberg describes Chicago on July 13th, 2005, when the temperature hit 106 degrees C, and felt like 126 degrees. In the following week, thousands of people rushed to emergency rooms with heat-related illnesses. Many died - 739 people above the expected deaths for the time of year. When government

---

[e] Page 213, tolerant nation, chambers quoting Harris and Startup: "...the story of Roman Catholics in Wales has been one of growth and consolidation, until 1970, after which decline set in.

interviewers tried to find out why, they found some patterns.

"Having a working air conditioner reduced the odds of death by 80%. Social isolation increased the risk. Living alone was particularly dangerous...Women fared far better than men, because they have stronger ties to friends and family. Despite high levels of poverty, Latinos had an easier time than other ethnic groups in Chicago...they tend to live in crowded apartments and densely packed neighbourhoods, places where dying alone is nearly impossible." (55)

Segregation and inequality seemed to play an important part in the death rates: eight of the ten communities with the highest rates were virtually all African American, with concentrated poverty and violent crime. However, three of the ten neighbourhoods with the lowest heat wave death rates were also poor, with high rates of violent crime and with predominantly African American locals, while another was mainly Latino. And these areas were even more resilient than Chicago's most affluent areas.

Klinenberg's wondering about this turned into the subject of his dissertation. He collected more data on the events, including speaking to people from 'matched' neighbourhoods – those with similar demographics, but with wildly different outcomes. He describes Englewood and Auburn Gresham, adjacent neighbourhoods on the south side of Chicago. 99% of residents from both are African American, and where poverty, unemployment and violent crime rates are high. Englewood's death rate during the heat wave was 33 people per 100,000 residents, whereas Auburn Gresham's was 3 people – making it one of the most resilient parts of the city.

With so many similarities, what explained the contrasting death rates? Klinenberg concluded that the main difference between the two areas was in their social infrastructure: the places where people can plan to meet, or simply bump into each other and have casual, unplanned conversations. Parks, shops, pavements, libraries, schoolyards, all provide opportunities for repeated interactions that develop strong social capital. When this happens, and, importantly, when people enjoy them, they tend to happen again, and relationships grow.

Residents of Auburn Gresham walked to diners, barbershops, parks, block clubs, church groups and grocery stores. People knew people, not because they set out to do that, but because the level of casual, social interaction was part of everyday life. During the heat wave, people checked up on each other, knocking on doors to make sure neighbours were OK. In reducing the risk of death in a heatwave, this social factor was equivalent to having a working air conditioner.

In Englewood, it was very different. The neighbourhood had been abandoned by business and by residents. Population had dropped by 50% between 1960 and 1990. The social infrastructure had decayed, and interactions became much less frequent. Neighbours didn't know neighbours, and social cohesion had withered.

Klinenberg concluded that these differences in social infrastructure were mainly predictive of the different outcomes. In Englewood, poor social infrastructure led to a loss of bonds between neighbours, which increased social isolation, and greatly raised the risk of death in this heatwave event. And the value of social cohesion was directly expressible in health outcomes, beyond the heat wave. Half a decade before the disaster, life expectancy in Auburn Gresham was more than 5 years higher than in Englewood. When he looked at other examples of matched pairs of neighbourhoods, Klinenberg found the same pattern: neighbourhoods that proved resilient during the heatwave were always safer and healthier than other places with similar demographics.

24: The Community group

A group of 6 women, meeting me in a community centre in the central park of the area. They'd invited me to talk with them, after a neighbourhood lunch event some weeks ago, in the local church hall. What struck me was their frankness and the clarity. And their willingness to say how things were and how they are now.

So, I'm talking about the '30s now. If someone wanted somewhere to live, they just got married. You make room for them, wouldn't you? I think that's why there's so much dementia today, because of people living on their own, whereas years ago, the grandparents would be there, they'd be doing the veg, or doing something. Whereas now they're in their houses, they haven't got nothing to do.

Families lived together, they did, you know. You wouldn't see any part of your family out on the road, you wouldn't. You'd make room in the house. But in the old houses, we used to have a parlour, a kitchen and what we call a back kitchen then. And as you say, if somebody, a member of your family - you just made room for them, in the house. My Gran, Grandfather, Auntie, 5 children and my mother lived in one house. And it was only two bedrooms. But we all managed. And we all just lived together.

People used to say, 'If you go to hospital, you go to hospital to die'. And there was no chapel of rest, or anything. It was in the house. Everybody was in the house. The other thing they used to say is 'Don't let me die in the workhouse', which was Mount Pleasant hospital. Well, it was the workhouse, for poor people, the very poor. It showed you didn't have anything at all. It was pride as well.

They'd grown up together. You knew the family. You knew what the conditions were and their circumstances. We had a family lived next door to us. They used to come and knock the door on a Sunday and say: 'Can my mother borrow a tin opener?' And we'd say 'Yes'. And then five minutes later they'd come in and say: 'Could my mother have a tin of pears to open?' Mrs W- would come with her cup: 'T-can I have a drop of milk?' 'Certainly Mrs W-'. I give her the milk.

She'd go a bit further: 'I spilt some, can you fill it up?' Well, we used to keep a tin opener, especially.

Do you remember the sweet shop that used to be opposite at St Joseph's school. And I used to go in there every morning. I don't know if any of the rest of you did. And buy Spanish root! it would last you forever. All the shops that used to be on Carmarthen Road. Well that's another thing that's changed, see. Like if you wanted a stamp, you had to go a post office. If you wanted something for medical you went to a chemist? Now, you can get all these things in Tesco. Because people would meet in those shops. And If you went to the shop, you'd see someone you knew and you'd have a conversation with them, and you know, you'd find out bits of gossip.

If you went to church, you could talk there. And you used to talk on the front doorstep. My mother would talk sitting on the wall, at the top part of Bryn-Melyn Street. Women used to sit on the windowsills then, and talk.

Like the woman living in two doors down from me. If you felt a bit what's-her-name, you could always knock on a door and go in and have a chat and she'd ply you with tea. But there's nothing like that now.

I can remember my mother saying - this is in the '30s now, mind - my brother had pneumonia, I was in her house with diphtheria. And the neighbours used to come in to sit for my brother so that she could have a rest and things like that. You had your family close at hand, but you didn't need them with the neighbours, did you? And to tell the difference - the way it is now. A gentleman living opposite me died. We didn't even know he was dead. And we don't know if he's buried to this day. We're just assuming that he is. And, I mean, they've lived in that house for about five years haven't they? And she knew all the neighbours around there.

But there you are, you know, things have completely altered, they have, around here. Druggies. Absolutely full of drugs. Yeah. they're putting them all around here to live. They don't care who they put to live around here. The council are putting them all in the flats. It's only

111

three-storey flats, three blocks. When they were built, they were supposed to be for older people. Well, obviously they've moved, and every one that goes empty, it's either they've been in prison, or they are on drugs. I took the police in my back bedroom window to watch them. Now I didn't know what a bong was. And I said to the policeman: 'Well, what are they doing – they've got candles!' The police said: 'It's a bong.' Well, I said, 'What's a bong?' That's what, they were taking the drugs.

But today, they all know what's happening, but they don't do nothing about it. It's the council are a lot to blame for that because they don't care. They're getting the money for it. And they don't care who they put here. And it's not fair on the decent people who live around here, because the mess that's around the place, and the council don't do anything about it.

My neighbour next door, she fell and broke her wrist. I've been living next door, I didn't know till the week after, and she come to the door. When I saw her, I wrecked her, mind. I played hell with her. I said, 'I live next door', I said, 'do you want me to take your bin out now or anything?' People don't do things like that, now see. They don't do it.

When I first got married, my husband - all he wanted to do was come and live in Swansea. He thought it was a wonderful place. Nice people. I've got to say that much about Swansea now. If you catch a bus, somebody always comes on to you, to talk to you. I've heard more life stories on the bus than anywhere. So, whether I've got a dull face, or they think, 'Oh, she looks alright.' But there's always somebody on the bus will come on and chat away I think on the whole, you know - Swansea - you get more good than bad.

25: Glen

'You should speak to Glen' my aunt had said. And now we're taking by phone. He grew up in Greenhill, and has maintained touch with the place throughout his life. His energy is crackling, and he has a hard-to-match recall for the place.

There was a community when we were young. The community was the local church. And you know 50 years ago there was the Bronman's, there was another church, mind, in Chapel Street. I knew the minister there very well, a man called Robert Thomas, wonderful man. And a lot of people went to that church, quite a few went to the Bronman's church. Coming to Greenhill Street, next to Brian Thomas' mother's aunt, Mrs Phillips, go up a flight of stairs and there on the left was Mr Bronman's Mission, Greenhill Mission, and that was said to be built by the men who had been in Martin Marney's lodge. Irish men, labourers who worked over there and helped them to dig the foundations and that.

When we were boys, you know, 16, 17, starting chasing around after girls and so on, we'd go into Citadelli's, have a coffee there, we could sit there for 2 hours having a chat over a cup of coffee. Then lower down on the corner of Matthew Street, there was another café and the boys would gather there you know on a Saturday or Sunday evening, boys from Matthew Street, boys from Swan Street, Powell Street, John Street, Greenhill Street. Cos we'd all, perhaps the day before, been playing football up in the Dyfatty park... And there's no community there now. No environment for children in any case, you know – there's even less for them to play with now than when we were boys there.

Don't forget - it's an aside but it's important - the Duke Public House, that was a big part of the community. Now the Full Moon was something different. The Full Moon was known as the Bucket of Blood and it's where you went if you wanted a fight. Mrs Evans, now her name wasn't Mrs Evans, it was MacIntyre, it was Mrs Evans originally, she married a chap who played rugby, called Phil Evans, but he died. She had 2 children with him…and when Phil died she kept it. But she didn't have much money, and she was running short I think, so she married a bloke called MacIntyre who was a seaman, and that poor bugger - everybody tells the tale of the night…he was a seaman, it was during the war, and she ordered a taxi for him, and it was a terrible night, pouring with rain and the rest of it, and she put him in the taxi to send him off to his ship, which she had to in any case because if you missed your boat during the war you were in serious trouble. And the poor bugger got drowned. His ship was torpedoed. She kept that pub going till it was knocked down. Now every St Patrick's Night there was a bloody big feast in there, a gathering, a big dance and a big do for St Patricks Night. They wouldn't have St David's night or anything like that but there'd be a St Patrick's Night. It would be the whole community.

These were the community meeting points. People did have a community, and a strong community. When someone died in that street, no strangers came into that house - it's either the son or the daughter or the niece who carried on living there in that house, so the whole family tradition went all the way down. For example, if someone died in Greenhill Street, a collection would be made in Greenhill Street, in Mill Street, in Chapel Street, in Green Row, and in the front of High Street. Why? Because everybody knew who had died.

And don't forget they'd come through the war. I was too young to remember the actual scenes and that, but I can remember my brother telling me, who's older than me, and my grandmother, incendiary bombs were dropping on the roof, you could hear them hit the roof, and rolling on to the road…There was all sandbags placed around the area. They were running out, getting the sandbags and throwing the sand on the bloody incendiary bombs, putting them out. This is what makes a community, Rob.

(Describing the housing clearances.) That's right – it was all knocked down – let me try and remember, '61 is when we left there – that's when they started knocking the houses out. That was a very sad time

for us because the writing was on the wall for us all to be thrown out. What happened there really was a bloody disgrace. The only man who fought for the people was man called Arthur Edwards and he did his best to fight for the people there, because what we were promised originally was that the streets would go one by one, and the people would be temporarily located somewhere else. The streets put back around the area and the people would come back and live there. These people had been promised for years: part of the houses got to go away because we got to build a swimming pool there. All bullshit: no swimming pool was never developed, was it?

They were considered to be slums weren't they and whilst they didn't have the facilities that you've got today, that's quite true. But you take for example Brian's grandmother's side – they were council houses – they were owned by the City Council, and they had big, long back gardens to them and they could have very easily have extended those houses by putting back kitchens on them with bathrooms and all the rest of it.

Our house, for example, my grandmother's house, my grandmother had it as a little boarding house. When I was a boy, my grandmother took in boarders in that house because to make a bit of money. My grandmother had a very big house, because as I said she took in boarders, we had 4 or 5 people living in our house. These houses, because they were so big, they could have been redeveloped and not knocking them all down.

But T- was one of those people who was easily led. I can remember him standing in Dyfatty when they opened the first block of flats, and I was there in the bowling green with the old men who were being shoved out of their homes around the area, looking sadly on. Some of them had ended up living on the Gors Road there, poor old buggers, walking back and fore now between the Gors and down to the park and sit there in the evening, or attend the Pensioners which is still there by the way. And T- gets up there and we are all listening, and he says 'It's a wonderful day today to be here to unveil the opening of these flats. Now I know lots of people don't like these

115

flats at all, but we haven't got enough land and it's not a bit of good getting hot-headed under the collar about it'. So that was his speech you see.

I remember a woman, she had a shop on High Street, Miss H-. I remember Mr B- who was a really nice man, he went in to Miss H's one day and he was complaining about some of the people in the area, and Miss H- said to him, 'Look here Mr B- whatever you say about this area, it's a very moral area. You'll see no red lamps here like you will down in Sketty.' Whether that was true about Sketty at that time or not, I don't know, but she put Mr B- in his place about the morality of Greenhill and the area.

I mean when we moved from there, I tried to get as near as I could to where I'd already been living – the nearest we could get for my father, my brother and myself, I wasn't married in those days, was to move to Town Hill. We had a house in Grosvenor Road, nice lounge, bathroom and so on, but our heart was never in it, never in it. Because we were townies as we were called, we were from Greenhill. All our neighbours who we knew all our lives, like Brian, and all the other boys, we all knew each other, and we'd all meet in town from time to time say 'How are things? How are you getting on? And all the rest of it. But the community was destroyed.

And it's so sad because I know several people died of a broken heart. One old chap played for Dyfatty, - his name was -. His parents were quite wealthy, they had several butchers shops. Now he was living in Croft Street, the first house when you come into Croft Street. Now that poor old bugger ended up living up in the furthest end of Gors Avenue on the road there you know, and he used to walk down to the park on a Saturday to watch the bowls, he was too old then, he was in his late 70s. They found that poor old bugger dead in that flat, you know, on his own. - the barber, now he had a barbers' shop in the High Street. He ended up on the main road up in the Gors on his own, nobody there, died there, ended up with dementia walking around all over the place, nobody knew anything about him.

Unfortunately, if I'd have had the knowledge that I had 3 or 4 years later, because I'd been developed by that time, I'd been active in the trade union movement, I could have given leadership at that level and been assistant perhaps to - who was trying to do some good. But I didn't have it at that time, and unfortunately nobody else did. Once you start moving one or two old houses, then get broken into, they get put on fire, all the rest of it, it's not long before everybody says, 'Let's get out of here'.

You'll never remake the dots – even if they rebuilt it all now, you can never have a community like it was. Because High Street is gone, Lewis' shop, John Bull's, McPhearsons', all the shops were there, they're gone. It's become a paradise for the prostitutes, the street walkers and the pedlars of drugs.

There is no community as such around there now, it's just people who are living there. It's somewhere to live and nothing else. When they wonder why Swansea has turned out as it is today, I've told these councillors - I go to any meetings there are and bawl them out. Until the High Street has got life in it, Swansea will never be a proper thriving city.

As a Greenhill boy it's not scary to me, I can always look after myself you know, but I mean, it could be scary if you don't know the area. You've got to be on your guard. One night I was on my own there in Greenhill Street, I was parked there and I'd lost my bloody car keys and it was pitch dark. And I'm bending down looking for my keys, and this woman appears in front of me, and she says to me 'Hello, are you looking for business?' 'No', I said, 'I'm looking for my fucking keys, piss off'. So you never know what you're going to see there. Some of these people you've got to address in a certain vernacular I'm afraid.

26: Pieces - How It Is

Taylor: My mother came to see me at Christmas and was fine, and she fell ill in about February time, and she didn't really say anything, but her neighbours in the street were absolutely fantastic in terms of taking care of her and looking after her and they did an amazing job. And I think in a way that certainly wouldn't happen in London... I mean it's dissipated. My mother doesn't really know her next door neighbour, or the people who live opposite, but there are still some people there that she is still closely connected to. They still ring up all the time. So that was very helpful, there's still a little bit of that left.

Katy: Oh we are in - Street, we are as strong. And I think in the Waun Wen area the majority of people are close. We've got people from Bangladesh across the road and they bought the houses that were built, remember the houses that were built in the square where the bombing was? Yes but one of them had bought that house and it's done up beautiful. The gentleman is from Bangladesh...I'm very friendly with them. Then there's neighbours in Auntie B-'s house and they are from the Philippines, and they call me Nana - and everything. Even the father calls me Nana - you know.

Morris: It's funny, my mother was... saying the other day a group of people who live down the road went up the park the other evening and every one of them was shouting over and asking me how she was and if there was anything they can do for her, which is lovely. I think a number of the people who moved into the area have had some relationship with the area previously, so there's a guy who lives a couple of doors down, a guy called -. And his daughter lives next door to him as well, and they're really good as well. There are a few other people who have moved into the area who are also very good so it's still not a bad place to be in fairness.

Sarah: Horrendous. That's why I moved up here because I lived in - Street, there was - Street where I lived of course and where you lived, and of course they were all privately owned houses then…next two houses up from me was sold to builders and they done them up and put youngsters in it, druggies, alchies. Oh the noise in the night and the people back and forth. I was frightened honestly. For about two years I struggled, and it was the same you know every other dotted house you know. There was only about three or four old neighbours left in my street when I left…that was really sad…and it was quite frightening. But then I was much older then. I was on my own, so yeah I didn't feel safe and secure down here at all.

Church support group: You know, when they come to church, a lot of the old elderly people are still coming to church. Well, I suppose, the young mothers now, they don't seem to be involved do they? We've got a little group of young mothers - I'm talking in their 30s. But they come occasionally and do something for the children…But they don't meet as a group in parish, do they? No, no no.

Priest 3: *…I came down for three days to speak to people…And I walked in there, and I was expecting to see maybe 20, 30 people but there were about 60 or 70, almost all women. And it was very striking, because I think, in some ways I think when I was growing up here, it was a bit of a matriarchy. The women organised a lot.*

It still is the same. It hasn't changed. The women are the centre of the life of the community.

How so?

Well, I don't know. Maybe you can dwell into the sociology of the people of Greenhill. Maybe looking at their Irish background, maybe, maybe. Maybe it has been an historical thing, that people just get used to. Maybe, maybe. But I think it's more of the sociology of the people around here, you know. About, you know, the way women always been the ones caring, and then really organising things. Nevertheless, we have the support of men, you know, sometimes the men at the background, really working at the background. But women are more in the limelight of getting things

119

done. But the men also they give tremendous support to all these activities…

Peter: They're all panicking about foreign immigrants, drugs. Rockland Terrace and bits and bobs, a couple of druggies living there, back and forwards over the last couple of years. I mean…I haven't been back to the street for 6-7 months, not even to walk past, I drive past in the car quite often on the main road…I walked down the Gors, and I take everybody as I find. But you do look and think: is there any need to be like that? And I look at it and think it's just not changed since I was a kid. It's still renowned - even the dogs walk in pairs around the Gors, for protection. And it doesn't feel, it's nowhere near the same, you don't know anybody there, I don't think they know each other's neighbours, don't know anybody else, but I just think that's the way society is these days.

Morris: Things just get older, people get older, in the end you don't tend to notice a lot changing. I think the whole thing as well of the community is obviously, dying is probably as good a word as you can use. In as much that, if I'm home go to church on Sunday with my mother then you see that the number of people going to church are fewer and fewer, probably because you go there and 50% of the people are older than us and by definition those guys are dying at some stage. And also, with the church social club not there as well, you lose contact with people. I think the social club closing was a terrible thing for people like my mother and –'s mother, and people of that age who don't really want to go anywhere else to replace it, but still enjoyed going down there to catch up with people they had known all their lives and to have a game of bingo.

Church support: We've had visitors from Australia come in, and Canada, to check up on their family histories. you know. So like, the parents, all the records are here, see. They lived around here at some point. And then they move to Australia and Canada and places like that. And that young girl, she, when she came over, I'm not sure, from Spain or something, about three or four months ago. And three of the children were baptised here, but she needed proof of a

120

baptism, because she was getting married abroad. And we found it. She didn't have much information, you know, but she needed proof of it. Remember those group of girls: three of them, I think they were, three sisters. They all came and we looked up all their records for them...Well, as you say, they've got to come back here for proof. You know, with the children making the Holy Communion now. They come: 'Oh, can we have a copy of a baptism certificate?' Because perhaps years ago they weren't issued with one you know, they were given like a candle or something like that...

Kevin: And, of course, the other thing is and what people seem to forget, is the cost structure of life have changed. In the 1920s or 1910's before the war, your wife didn't work, you worked, you came home, gave her housekeeping, and went down the pub. Or you went to have a haircut and talked to your mates or what have you, that all changed, that changed in the 50s and 60s and progressively now in the 70s more dramatic change. So, the cost structure of life changed, both husband and wife worked, and then as time has gone on, because of the pressure of life and pressure of costs, pubs have closed down because people couldn't afford to go to them.

Priest 3: Well, I still carry the responsibility...it has not changed from the role of Father Richards - I still see myself as being available for people to come to. It's difficult times now, really, and it's a changed world altogether. But then I still make myself available for people. I still see myself as a symbol of hope, a symbol of unity and it's just being a priest, for them - all things to all Men, in the combination. And they still have this, kind of a, regard for you, as a priest. Although some, which is the case, some will ignore you, some will look at you with pity and some will also see you as being there for them. But, the bottom line is, if there is any difficulty or challenges that people are facing, it comes back to me and I need to respond to that.

Simon: ...the sorts of things that we did when I was a kid and a teenager, you couldn't get away with doing now. Health and safety, all the stuff we did about constructing aerial runways and all the rest of it, would all be far too dangerous. You go somewhere where it's done professionally, where they've got insurance, and then rightly of course people have got to be approved to be around kids. All those things are necessary, but the effect of that is the people who would get involved, go 'Oh I'm not doing that, it's too complicated'. There are two blokes down the Sandfields, the kids wanted play football, there's nowhere they could do it, so they've started a junior league. Now, we were having the discussion a few weeks ago, what's going to happen to it when those kids who are now coming at the end of their time to be able to play, because they're now at secondary school, and you know, it's the little kids they were talking about, you know the 6 and 7 year olds. Who's going to take that over? And that provides something in the community where people get to meet. Loads of those things just don't happen anymore.

Kevin: Yes, volunteering is a very difficult and a very precarious occupation these days because of the various issues surrounding insurance liabilities and the willingness of people to go to a solicitor if little Johnny falls over playing football or rugby or running or whatever. Youth clubs find it very, very difficult to have community liability because parents are willing to sue at the drop of a hat, and there is always an issue about public liability and the way in which people are approached. And on top of that many people used to volunteer because they had time on their hands, or they had good jobs, or jobs that they didn't need to work overtime, or they worked Monday to Friday, that type of thing. But, of course, life has changed dramatically in as much as the working week now is 5 out of 7 and as such you could be working every Saturday and Sunday, and you might organise a junior football team now but you can't now because they play on a Saturday, so you know the whole emphasis of volunteering has changed as well.

Priest 3: When I think about the stories I heard from people about Greenhill, it used to be a, kind of, a strong community, but I don't really feel that sense of community again. And I don't think it's just about Greenhill, I think it's just a modern-day thing. But then, at the same time, people still come back to it, people still have the sense of

122

belonging and that is why you have so many people would want their funerals to be done in St Joseph's, because they still have their seeds in Greenhill, as part of their life, an integral part of their life, fundamental to them. So, they always come back, even when they are dead....

They always come back, even when they're dead?

Yes! Yes, because they want their funeral from St Joseph's, that's what I mean. They want to come back to the St Joseph's cathedral, you know? And just talking about the centre of everything in Greenhill in the past, it used to be St Joseph's. We talk about the 60s and perhaps 70s...Maybe, it began in the 1800s, St Joseph's was the centre of everything. So, that's why they still want to come back.. It's like a gateway to heaven.

Church support: Have you been in the crypt?

I've never been in the crypt

Right. It's worth going down because people's ashes are in here. Boxes I call them. I'm ending up in a box - our husbands are down there already. We used to have Brownies in there. We used to have Cubs with the boys. And when we had the hall years ago, when we used to have a youth club. Table Tennis and you know…

27: Dad's end

I remember Dad having once said that he'd been happier in my earlier years. Things had been simpler when we were young children. They began to fall apart later in our less compliant years. He'd lost some control, was hurt, and backed off, turned away.

In the months after my sessions with Jan, equipped with more energy and enough detachment, I understood that my parents hadn't been close for a long time. And that, as a kid, I knew it in my body without being conscious of it. That the closeness to my mother was always strong, though imbued with vague intimations of loss. With Dad it was simpler and clearer. We'd been close but parted in defiance. I'd been ready for something new, anything new. And he was tired of trying to shake me up, and of my opposition. We needed a break from each other, and that break lasted around twenty years. Now I was starting to imagine a different way of being with Dad – more direct and less rebuking. Perhaps with more kindness for each other.

Their divorce had hit him hard. Mam had wanted to leave him, and he was desperately hurt, ashamed and angry. He retreated into his thoughts and back to his chair, like his father before him. He didn't come to my wedding in 1998 – he couldn't face it, knowing she'd be there.

When Dad came to Mam's funeral, they'd been divorced for eight years. As our car stopped outside the church there was an enormous thunderclap, which lifted everyone's spirits: she might be gone, but she still had a view about things….

Perhaps his loneliness, and my maturing, helped us appreciate each other a little more. In the years either side of Mam's death, I understood that the closeness with my mother had ripples with my father. After what had come before, he'd probably been a bit sidelined in those early years. We don't know what we're born into, and my arrival disturbed the patina of our own potent history.

Now, he began to share more about his own life. in particular, his relationship with his father helped me understand him, and this changed how I thought of him. At the Waun Wen Inn, we sat, over a pint: "He never liked me", he told me, still with a genuine confusion after all this time, but no self-pity. I was reminded of those childhood Sunday visits to his father. Four decades on, and the pieces were cohering. Being the tender-hearted scrapper he was, over the years, he'd absorbed deeply the feelings of hurt and confusion and had developed a restless, vigilant, spring-loaded response-ability. He used to talk so little about himself, but now something had changed.

And some things remained the same. On these short visits, he'd still offer me unsolicited and pointless advice. On his side-table, beside the many issues of *Ireland's Own*, he'd push my way a copy of *The Grocer* magazine. "Some very good jobs in there, Robert. Very good Manager jobs..." When he was back on his advice-horse, he felt good and strong. I nodded and read the ad. Our differences were momentary, surface shimmerings.

***

As a young man he played a lot of football, like most of his brothers. During his national service he continued playing. In one match he was whacked on the shin by a local farmer and carried off the pitch. The medical officer at the nearby army camp told him he may have sprained his foot, and after a month he was walking again. At 56, working for the city council, he slipped during his work, hurting the same leg. The x-ray showed an old fracture. And this new wound would plague him for the next eight years. In the end he chose amputation over ongoing pain and painkillers.

18/01/99: Dad had his operation on Wednesday 6th. He's had his right lower leg removed, three inches below the knee. It all happened quickly. Pain, in to see Dr O'Kane. Passed to Morriston hospital. X rays, wait over new year, till Dr Downs appears and then prognosis: off. He's a strong one. He bears his bad news. It certainly doesn't seem to get him down too much and for too long. So, physiotherapy for arms, upper body and leg strength. Orthopaedics for the leg fitting. Convalescence.

I visited Dad, on Carmarthen Road, where he was now living alone. We'd been concerned about Dad's memory. He'd been forgetful, and repeating himself, so we contacted his GP, and he was due today. When the doctor arrived, I walked him through to the lounge where Dad sat in his chair. He administered the 30-question survey: What time is it? What's the date? Who's the Prime Minister?... Dad got 28/30 correct.

"You've done well, but I think we'll take you in for a scan, Mr Sheffield", said the doctor. He meant a brain scan. As we left, I took the doctor out through the kitchen to the back garden exit. As we passed the hob, we both saw that one was still burning on a low setting. Dad had left it on after cooking his breakfast, earlier that morning. We looked at each other and I turned it off. The scan confirmed what we suspected. He had significant brain shrinkage.

"I don't have that forgetting illness do I, Bob?" he asked me soon afterwards. I couldn't tell him the truth.

Alzheimer's progresses in a both steady and stop-start way. We moved Dad from home to St James, a controlled accommodation in the Uplands. He was declining, but still determined to follow his routines and lead a life recognisable to himself. And while we wanted him to eke out whatever quality of life he could, Paula and I agonised about balancing his freedom with his safety. Distance-monitoring of parents is difficult, and we wondered how his days were spent. Through a network of neighbours and friends, we pieced together that he'd visit the pub at lunchtime for a couple of pints, spend some time in Treasure, a favourite café, have an ice cream from Joe's, and spend some time by the sea. His routines were very important to him. They eased his scratching anxieties.

One week, he fell down three times, including once from a moving bus, giving himself two black eyes and a cut nose. We realised that he'd need more intensive care, and we moved him into St John's care home in Cwmbwrla. He was accepting of it, and touchingly trusting of our efforts. Though, here again, his motion compulsions would soon manifest. We set up another loose federation of watchers and reporters, including care home staff, pub staff, and local friends. The staff from St Johns were patient and understanding, and would sometimes walk him home from a local pub, having let him finish his pint. And sometimes, his friends would take him for a walk, a drink, and even a sing:

When he was in St Johns, he was absconding a lot, wasn't he? (Bill)

To the local pubs?

And the Cwmfelin club. (Bill)

Yeah, he was. And to the Malsters, nearby. Me and Paula used to get in touch with the landlords, so they would let us know if he turned up there.

You know once, I went down there, and funnily enough, right, I used to go and see him when he was in St Johns. And that was at Christmas time, and I'd had a couple of pints. They had a guest singer there, his name was K- and he was at school with me, and he was a good singer. He was with a group... Anyhow, I goes down and me and Don had a drink there, drinking because it was Christmas...we had a good drink. You know the patients, all from Greenhill...And I started singing Irish songs, the place was bouncing, they were up dancing! And this K-, he was right put out, because he was getting paid, we were taking all the shine! Great, it was. (Bill)

13/10/2009: reflecting on a weekend at centre parcs in Longleat. A French woman described time as 'sand in my hand' in some recent piece. As I was sitting outside our cabin listening to the lush life of the forest – birdsong, wind, squirrels expecting food... - a thought arrived that dementia is a little like the forest getting quieter and less busy. Less lifely.

He was gradually diminishing, and the staff at St Johns told us that he'd need more specialist care, from a dedicated dementia care home. We'd have to move him again.

20/06/2010: I went with Paula today to visit 2 care homes for people with dementia... Which brought up old feelings of betrayal. Him of me, me of him. Round and round the mulberry bush...

By now, added to his advanced dementia, he'd also developed Parkinson's. We moved him into Castle Craig, where he had excellent

127

care, the people, as ever, making all the difference. The team was led by Sabah, who had compassion to burn and a team which was clearly with her. By now, our second child had been born, and I visited with the full family when could.

18/10/2010: the past is never far away but we have found a happy place now though. At the end of each visit, he is always surprised to hear me say that I live in Bristol now. "Oh?..."... I'm now trapped in the iron-grip of his long-term memory, and my childhood seems to have lasted so long.

Stuart Jeffries, a Guardian journalist says that children think that nothing changes whereas grown-ups know that everything changes. "Time is nothing, son", Dad said to me around this time, but he is talking more about himself, I imagine: how can memories so fresh be so far away?

6/8/2010: from the terrace of the pool at the Essex inn in Chicago: Big Pink are playing "Dominoes" on the lake shore opposite at the Lollapalooza festival.

17/8/10: (Flying to Helsinki): the meaning of middle age is to be torn between different worlds. And sometimes to be caught, surprised by a tune. In this case, "Christmas is a comin'" by Leadbelly. Christmas, like shrapnel, will find your soft parts.

8/7/12: I leaned close to him and whispered: "Do you know me?". "Of course I know you", in a voice which is a breath.

His tea is too milky, and he doesn't like it.

"I have to go, Dad. Back to Bristol, to do some work."

"Flippin' heck. Already?"

His face shows no emotion - ...Parkinson's mask conceals. He raises his hand and wafts me away, with an imperial power. He still feels hurt, can still feel sorry for himself, still has pride, as well as a sense of himself and other.

In the early months of 2016, it becomes increasingly clear that it's the final few months for Dad. We've been through it before, Paula and me, and there was something familiar about the pattern: increasing hospital visits, weight loss, lack of appetite, and a lack of pleasure.

Paula would visit him several times a week, to be with him, and sometimes to feed him. Towards the end, he started to turn his face away from the spoon. Paula and I talked about it: what was happening, and how to get round it? And then we realised this was his final decision. Whatever awareness of his world he had left, he was telling us something important. We were struck dumb with sadness and then with resigned admiration. Perhaps thoughts of choice and survival are the last to go, even with Alzheimers.

At home, I'd booked a flight to Sri Lanka over Easter, leaving on Friday 25th March. Of course, as the date draws nearer, so the inevitable becomes clearer. Paula and I talk about whether I should postpone the holiday. We agree that there's no point, nothing to be gained, and what will happen will happen.

I visit Dad to say goodbye on Thursday 24th March. He is shrunken, tiny, not himself, still himself. And holding his hand, I tell him that I love him and I've always loved him, and I'm sorry about what happened, and I don't understand it. I keep holding his hand and the tears come. And he looks at me steadily and calmly, his usual shaking gone. On the way out, I looked around his bare room at the stuff we'd need to collect in the coming weeks. A couple of shopping bags of clothes, two Welsh rugby DVDs, an Elvis CD, a few family photos, a wood and brass catholic icon. And, in the main lounge area, daffodils, as Easter weekend was approaching.

***

At the funeral, there was a good gathering of his friends and family. My old friends, Paul and Ed, turned up to give support at the St Joseph's church service. The ceremony was a blur, and I felt hollowed out by a long spoon. Presiding over everything was the conviction that we were bringing him back home, and that's what he'd have wanted.

After the ceremony, we drove to the burial plot, where I saw Sabah, with some of her team from the care home. I thanked them for coming. She looked tired. She'd decided to take a break from the work, and she'd be moving back to her home up north for a while.

129

Later, at the reception, Dad's friend, Adrian, touched my arm softly and said: "He was a very close friend of mine, and there was no side to him at all."

15/04/16: It's Friday, 2 days after Dad's funeral. It's evening time, around 18.30 and I lay in bed, shattered. My father's face appears to me, clear and young – in his 40s. Calm and with an easy smile, his green-grey eyes shining. "Dad?...Dad?..." I call quietly, in my mind. My eyes are closed and I'm looking at his expression of peacefulness.

His death was a relief. For him, his friends and for us, his family. He'd endured the conflagration of his illnesses with typical determination and lack of complaint. And then it was time to go. And he wanted to go – that was clear to us. It felt a due ending. Over the previous fifteen years we'd both softened, dropped our flinty antagonisms, and became more open to the other. We accommodated each other in doses small enough for comfort, and big enough for something new to grow. Grand-children had helped - another triangle. In the end the differences meant less than what we shared.

28: The shift, the blight and the policy response

It turns out that others did think as I'd dimly recalled: this was a time and place with strong ties between people. The social cohesion developed without a plan, but because of the intentions and efforts of thousands of people. The area became a distinctive presence in the city. In its rousing, formative early years, it integrated immigrant Irish people with the local Welsh and with relatively little rancour. People in the area won battles for the growth of the physical infrastructure of housing, roads, a church, a school and a social club. All of this brought a psychological stability of long-term spiritual peace for the self, mid-term educational betterment for the next generation, and the short-term pleasures of meeting in the many different social settings that were available in the area.

These institutions and the neighbourhood itself also gradually developed the social infrastructure that gave many ways for children and adults to meet each other: church services and gathering outside the church before and after mass; church community groups; the social club, open 7 nights a week; the school gates and school volunteering; street pavements outside shops, the shops themselves, and homes, some of which were also shops; pubs, windowsills, doorsteps, street corners, cafes, barbers, green spaces, parks and more. And because many children living in the area went to local schools, those children would also encounter each other outside of school.

People enjoyed the kindnesses and pleasures of each other's company, which led to more interactions. This was the social and cultural essence of the area. The neighbourhood developed a distinct Welsh-Irish culture, which became a way of everyday life for people in the community. Despite inevitable urban challenges and changes, the area remained culturally distinct for more than a hundred years, from the mid-1800s to around the 1980s.

131

And the cohesion of the neighbourhood brought many benefits, that were felt in many ways, every day, by people living there. The feeling of being in a type of extended network of familiar people was reflected in low crime levels and a sense of safety; as well as financial, practical and emotional support; and a place where people could play, explore and simply be.

From the late 1950s through to the late 1970s, local government decisions contributed to the weakening of social ties in Greenhill. First, the demolishing of housing that moved people to other parts of the city. And second, the widening of Carmarthen Road, that removed the shops that gave the main opportunities for informal talk in the neighbourhood. Together, these decisions removed ways in which people met people. And because the interactions lessened, so did the bonds that gave the area its strength.

***

But it's not fair to lay everything at the door of local government. In the wider Western world, similar patterns were being seen. Puttnam reviewed levels of social capital in the USA from post-1945 to 2000 and found a consistent decline over this time. He listed these factors, from the least to the most important contributors:

- Pressures of time and money, including those for two-career families.
- Commuting, sprawl and suburbanisation increasing the time spent travelling to work.
- Electronic entertainment, including television, leading to private time becoming more personal, less social.
- Generational change, with a more civic-minded post-second world war generation, being succeeded by children and grand-children who 'are less embedded in community life'. (56)

All of these wider factors are relevant for Greenhill, and have been mentioned, directly or indirectly by people in this book. While local decisions certainly accelerated the area's fragmentation, the trend to a weakening of social ties would have continued anyway, but more slowly. While roads, shops and housing change suddenly, the effect of the weakening of social bonds takes longer. In Greenhill, because of the strong loyalties of a minority of remaining people, it's taken decades for their absence to be exposed. The writer and activist, Jane Jacobs, described the warning signs:

> "Stagnation and dullness is the first sign of an incipient slum, long before blight is visible. The young, the ambitious, the energetic, the affluent, desert the area. The area always fails to attract newcomers by choice." (57)

And now, crime levels, drug use and prostitution have increased, and perceptions of safety have declined, especially around the top end of High Street. Now, the area is more of a place to pass through than to be. Traffic slices west to east, through the crossroads of Dyfatty street to Bridge Street, and south to north, along High Street and Carmarthen Road. People walk by, mainly on their way to other places.

Perceptions of space matter to health and well-being. In Philadelphia, Eugenia South and her research team looked at the effect of creating small green spaces in poor, urban neighbourhoods. (58) They gathered 12 people - 8 men, 4 women, all African American, mostly older, with incomes under $15,000. And they asked them to do two walks, both within an area of two blocks of their home, while wearing Garmin monitors to track heart rates.

On the first walk, the group passed open, untreated empty lots – the kind of places associated with increased crime. While they did this, and despite these locations being familiar to the walkers, their heart rates rose by an average of 9.5 beats per minute. The team was concerned about these results, noting that living near to such areas generated recurrent stress, and changes in cardiovascular, neurological and endocrine systems over a lifetime for people exposed this way. To avoid all this, locals were more likely to choose not to walk at all, thus reducing the type of essential exercise for well-being.

133

On the second walk, two months later, they walked past empty lots that had been converted into small, accessible gardens, with trees and other vegetation. This time, average heart rates dropped. South and her team concluded:

"The reduction in heart rate suggests a biological link between vacant lot greening and reductions in acute stress."

Too much of the space around Dyfatty feels wasted and unsafe. Consciously or not, walking there is likely to be stressful for residents and visitors, and will be avoided, reducing human interaction, and making it even more unsafe. The area has long been economically poor and working class, and this remains. What has changed is the decay of support structures that people enjoyed for a hundred years. There are plenty of pockets of strong relationships, kindness and consideration between neighbours at street level. But the cross-generational reservoir of goodwill that spanned the neighbourhood has now frayed.

***

These times of community cohesion and fragmentation are recognised more widely in Wales.

"Wales needs strong, resilient and harmonious communities that can respond effectively to the increasing pace and scale of economic, social and cultural change in the 21st century."

So said the 2009 Welsh Government report, Getting on Together, a Community Cohesion Strategy for Wales. This and subsequent policy documents show a concern for addressing loneliness and social isolation, especially for older people. As well as recognising that place-based communities are becoming increasingly diverse, and that there is potential for differences to be exploited by far-right extremism. And the policy notes research that highlights how poverty and deprivation can be associated with lower community cohesion.

This document and later ones translated policy into goals, programmes and measures since then. Community cohesion remains a key government focus. All of this in an ideological context where

134

Wales is believed to have been traditionally good at building communities and welcoming outsiders. "Connect is the magic word", said a Gwent citizens panel in October 2019, with a nod to the increasing importance of digital connections. (59)

All of this is relevant for Greenhill, where there are echoes of its immigrant past. In 2010 Swansea became the UK's second city of sanctuary, welcoming people escaping war, violence, or persecution. A proportion of these people have been relocated into the Greenhill area, whose population rose from 1462 to 1792 between 2010 and 2020. That's an increase of 22.6% - one of the highest in Swansea for the period. (60)

The people who now live there are a mix. Some describe an older population clinging to a diluted way of life. Some are the sons or daughters of people with long-held connections to the place. Other people have left, for different places and opportunities. Some residents have moved there from outside, and don't share the same set of inter-generational family bonds, nor a historical awareness of the locality. Why would they?

Students are a major source of seasonal migration to Swansea. Just over 20,000 come to the university, arriving and departing at predictable times through the year. A student accommodation block has recently been built at the Seren building outside the railway station, just south of old Greenhill. And St Joseph's became the city's first primary sanctuary school in 2019, following an exploration of the journey of immigration of Irish to the area, and of the people who welcomed them. The school collaborated with artists Mandy Lane and Bill and Rachel Taylor-Beales. And the resulting work was shown in Tate Modern, London, Taliesin, Swansea and the Senedd, Cardiff. The school is much more ethnically diverse than when I was there as a child, and its pupils live across the city.

And the income-deprived Greenhill faces plenty of post-pandemic challenges. A 2020 report by the Joseph Rowntree Foundation pointed out that 25% of Welsh people lived in poverty, pre-COVID - a figure that had stood for a decade. And the poor risk being disproportionately affected. Low pay sectors have been most ravaged by COVID, with many jobs being lost. Rental housing risks being unaffordable, and parents are caught in a childcare trap, whose provision depends on working a minimum set of hours per week – precisely what the pandemic prevented. (61)

Where once the neighbourhood protected itself against the worst effects of poverty, local government now applies official efforts and resources to renew the area, counter the crime levels, and improve perceptions of safety. And then came the tempest of COVID-19, revealing the economic and social divides, and prompting a response from officials and locals. Teachers, priests, support staff, council workers, political councillors, voluntary sector employees and local residents are working in the place to bring about social, cultural and economic regeneration.

29: Teachers 2 and 3

One of the teachers has just given me a tour of the school – my first in 43 years. Physically, the corridors, the walls, the whole space, seem...disconcertingly and crushingly, exactly the same! Socially and culturally, it has changed a great deal. The teachers are describing this shift, including the school's adoption of Sanctuary School status, and the recent work to bring the past to the attention of current pupils and teachers.

Teacher 3: Well, I would say it's changed an awful lot, again coming back to it... When I first started here the people I taught did steep from that Irish immigration route. A lot of them had Irish heritage. We would go up to the cathedral or the Cenotaph outside and children would point to names on the war memorial saying, 'They're related to me, and they're related to me...'.

Teacher 2: Those conversations would be interesting in the office because they'd always be, 'Oh, you know so and so, down the road or down here'. And I would stand there, not being from Swansea myself, thinking, 'Oh my Gosh, how does everybody know each other?' Because people just did. And you were talking generations at a time.

Teacher 3: I think that is what has changed most because now most of our children seem to come from many other locations rather than from the close-knit Irish or Welsh communities that once were settled here in Greenhill and made up our school population.

Teacher 2: But Wales is also very different to when I worked in England because we had a high turnover of staff, people moved an awful lot, very ambitious and moved schools a lot. Whereas here, - is not unique in being here 25 years. And lots of people have come here to school as a child, or been to Bishop Vaughan school, and come back to the same area. I think that's quite uniquely Welsh. I don't think you see that in England."

Teacher 3: Again, when I first started here the immediate community would worship in the Cathedral as well. There was a lot more socialising of the school with the community, with the people who would attend the cathedral and who lived nearby. So, in St. Joseph's Catholic club, we would often have school events there. There would be a meeting of people from the local Parish and the school, in that way the school community was a lot more localised. I would say, the majority of my class at that point, even though they've always been bussed into school there was a much greater sense of, 'This is our community, this is our church' as many of them could trace back generations of their family that had attended the school. Now I think that children and their families are not just spread out more by location but by culture and place of origin also and as a result that essence of one shared Irish-Catholic community has been lost a bit, changed I would say.

When I started, so that would have been 94', there was one Asian family in the school, and that was it for the whole of the school. And now, we're 40% plus ethnic minority. And the dynamics have completely changed, for the better in many ways, in the fact that we are much more open and tolerant and accepting of diversity. There's been a massive shift, I would say, just in the time I've worked here to where we are today and how we approach the work that we do today and how that has changed throughout the time. So, there is a bringing together, through the school, of more communities, possibly of those that are fragmented, and ones that have national, religious and cultural differences. Sometimes they'll be smaller communities and they won't have the emotional connection for this particular geography as others in the community do for seeing it as home.

Catholicity is what will drive, in particular I would say, those Indian and Filipino communities and some of our Polish families as well. They're our three biggest, sort of, sub-communities, I would say. Many of our Indian families originate from Kerala, in Southern India. These along with many members of our Filipino community are people who have migrated into the area, because work has brought them here. A lot of our parents work often in the hospital, or care industry.

And so, with the migration of these communities, that within themselves are very cohesive, you get a blend of cultures. You know, the Indian and the Filipino families in particular celebrate together in their separate communities. They have festivals, often their parents will pick other children and siblings up and there is a lot of shared responsibility within their communities. And so, I think that's where the nature of our school has changed, the dynamics within it, embracing a more multicultural, blended approach.

We've got such a big Catholic-Indian community, so they will want to send their children to a Catholic school, which is important to them, and they will also worship in the Catholic parish which is nearby rather than St Joseph's. This means you can get splintered groups within one community, that actually work together, that are still very cohesive and supporting of each other. We also have very big Polish and Filipino communities that are very close-knit and bound together through their relationships, culture, faith and the school.

Teacher 2: I think we've got a lot of people needing social housing, which is up in Mayhill, Townhill area, that side. So, that will bring then people with children. And then you've got the areas on Llangyfelach Road, and some of Cwmbwrla and some of Manselton, where some of the asylum seekers are housed, so that's why they're coming to us because they don't have cars, they need to find a school where they can walk to. But, they all have an extremely strong work ethic, they all are extremely supportive of the school and what the school stands for.

Teacher 3: The school is the hub, teaching the values and traditions of and for the Catholic church. In doing so, it unites those different groups and communities, those that are fragmented and displaced, people seeking sanctuary, finding their way and who may feel like they do not have communities they feel that they belong to. In this way the school becomes that first point of contact and then through that, the teaching of faith, religion and of the Catholic church. Sometimes for some of our pupils and families seeking sanctuary, the religious emphasis is secondary, and it is that feeling of acceptance, of support, the way that they are welcomed which is of primary importance. And so it's sort of two-fold, isn't it? Because the church is there and we are, as the school, really feeding the church, but actually the church will feed the school as well. It's symbiotic."

I was quite a bit disillusioned with the job a couple of years ago. And I was really feeling a bit burnt out and thinking, 'Oh, my gosh, like, it's just a bit mundane'. You know, I suppose it was that part of my career where I felt a bit stuck. And then I started doing the Arts Council Lead Creative Schools project and this led to new projects in Expressive Arts and, it's really sort of invigorated me again, and I just love it.

The art piece 'Journey' was created as part of a Lead Creative Schools scheme funded by the Welsh Government and Arts Council of Wales. We started working with Swansea City of Sanctuary to welcome sanctuary seekers into our community. It began through our study of Irish immigration and was lovely because, even though lots of our children don't personally have this heritage, it is why our school is here and so through school it becomes part of shared heritage of education and faith. When we started off the project we started looking at an art focus, where should we do our trail and one of the children said, 'We should go to the Cathedral and we should look there'. So we did that and we started then looking at the history of the cathedral, looked inside, saw the shamrocks, started digging around, thinking 'What was here before, why are we here?'

We discovered there was a really cohesive community of people who lived here. Actually, I would say all our children who participated, regardless of their faith or their cultural background, now have a very good sense and understanding of why we are here and who came before. They know that children lived here and walked barefoot to Mass and knew that people worked in the Hafod, lived in Greenhill and the surrounding area, paying a penny a brick to build the cathedral. Before our project we were in danger, I suppose, of

140

losing that story a little bit...losing the heritage of our school, local community and cathedral, losing the hidden stories of the Irish immigrants in the 1850's. The stories are ones of great destitution and desperation, of faith and community and of hope and education. Stories that certainly shouldn't be lost and never retold.

But in this project, journey is more than this. It is really about a bringing together of people, a journeying of everybody's route. The result of the initial work we did took us on a different path, one looking at migration of people and sanctuary. We used different art forms and this began our journey looking at what a haven is and how we can be that for people in our communities. So then we then worked on writing a song, constructing a sculpture, making artwork for all with this theme and we invited our asylum seeker parents and refugee families in to work on it with us...

In 2018, from the 548 schools that took part in this initiative we were one of only 32 schools chosen to showcase our work in the Tate Exchange, at the Tate Modern in London. 'Journey' also formed part of Swansea Museum's 'Our Abertawe' exhibition, was installed in Taleisin Art Gallery and as part of the 'Let's celebrate' festival was one of only three projects to go into the Senedd.

It's important in a school because then those children you know, you learn about the forgotten stories of the past and not always the ones that people remember. You consider people's, individual journeys, but also that it makes you reflect on your own and then the future. But certainly the project that went to Tate Exchange and the Senedd, focus on a forced migration and immigration. There's one beautiful image of just the clasped hands of children on the beach...And, so the art moves from Irish immigration in the late 19th century and then it comes full circle making it relevant still today, giving it a very modern twist.

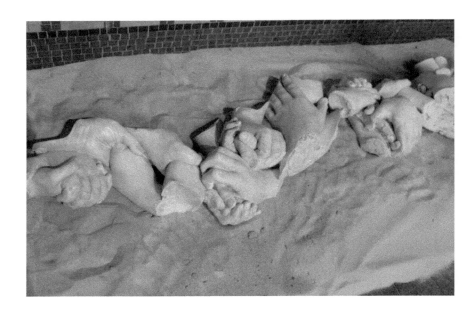

30: The Local Workers

Four workers from different sectors, and in different roles, who all work in the locality, trying to make it a better place to be. They describe their work, pre, during and post-COVID, and the futures they want for the area.

Simon: In Swansea 30% of houses are social housing, 30% of adults have no formal qualifications…We have the highest proportion in Wales of children living in workless households. Life expectancy is 13 years less in the east of the city compared to the affluent west of the city. We know all these things, so we know that the people in Greenhill are all in those categories.

Jane: And we're trying to pull the communities back together, really. But it isn't easy. It's very close to city centre. And therefore, it comes with lots of poverty, lots of people who perhaps live in the high blocks, the high block flats there, that come with their own complexities and their own difficulties…there's people that have lived there all their lives. And they want it back safe. … And there's other people that have moved there and haven't got the same respect for the area. Don't know the area, don't feel they owe anything to the area. It's very close to the train station, and therefore, the county lines with the drugs, you know, that is their first port of call…We've got a large proportion of the community that are very vulnerable. There's no two ways about it.

Simon: You know, pubs would have cricket teams and football teams. I mean there hardly any pubs left in Greenhill. And that's what's missing, is active hubs within the community…so the church and the men's club, and the pub, and the shops, and all the rest of it, people would meet in the post office and everything. Well, all of those things that work in the community and kept the community together have gone…the council has such limited resources now, it's directing its attention to the areas of the most obvious, greatest need…the loudest voice works, and we've tried to be the loudest voice for those communities.

Jane: We're trying to change the picture there. That narrative is shifting, definitely. So we're hugely concentrating on that partnership work with the community…And what we're trying to do is support people so they feel welcomed in the community. So they feel it is their home, and that they have got people that care about them… So we were trying also to change the sort of physical look of the area as well and bring work into the area. And bring student accommodation in... As you come to the traffic lights, at the top of Dyfatty, on the right there, you've got a row of, derelict shops. So, we've just taken over those now, and we've had grant funding, we're converting them into units for that area. Employability will be there. The NHS will be there. Substance misuse. Sexual health. We want to run courses from there for people.

We want to have an area that is safe, so people can come in and drop in. What we realise is the fact that it takes a long time to build relationships with people. They don't trust you, just because you've got a badge around your neck, and you say: 'You can trust me'. You have to build those relationships. And therefore, if there's somewhere where the kettle's always on, and they get used to seeing the same faces, and the same people.

The volunteer element there is just beyond anything, I have to say. And if anything has really shone a light, it's been COVID…And just across the road from the train station, you've got Matthews House - the work they've done has been unbelievable. The support for people having food, people being given drinks, people been given clothes, you know. Because many people are afraid to come to the authorities. They're afraid to say: 'I'm sleeping on somebody's settee'. But they're not afraid to go out somewhere like Matthew's house. They build up that trust. And then the team will introduce them to us in a helpful way, an informal way. And then we can help people where they perhaps wouldn't necessarily have just come to the local authority and said, 'I need help'.

We've got new roles here in Swansea and they're called local area coordinators. And their skills are pulling that community together. Perhaps meeting with a vulnerable person or somebody lonely. And introducing them to other people, and groups. And their roles have taken off brilliantly. And COVID really brought them out. And they're almost like that glue in the community...involved in a lot of the men sheds, and different light-touch mental health support groups. It could be a walking group, it could be a coffee morning[f], where people just get to know each other and talk. Sometimes people just need that bit of encouragement or support to go to group. To join. After that they're away, aren't they?

Andrew: It wasn't just working with public sector partners, but with the third sector, community groups, and we had an amazing response from Swansea residents to volunteer... Our Local Areas Coordinators played a significant role to co-ordinate local activities and make sure that those who are the most vulnerable get all appropriate support...This connected us within the communities as people get on well in their neighbourhood by speaking and chatting with each other more frequently and this changed the whole community dynamics. During COVID-19 restrictions we have noted that our weekly hate crime cases were significantly low. That was something very positive and this may be due to lack of interactions with each other or could be due to the increase social capital in our communities or because all of us were fighting against a new phenomenon that no one had experienced previously.

Tony: During COVID we brought a collaborative effort of 50 organisations and charities together to form Swansea together with a mission "To do our best to remember the vulnerably housed"...

---

[f] Coffee can have a role in community cohesion. In the working-class cafes of Naples, early in the nineteenth century, began the tradition of the *caffè sospeso* - the suspended coffee. On paying the bill for coffee, a person would pay for two coffees: one for the next person who might need it but not be able to pay. Over time, the practice ebbed and flowed, according to times and need, becoming a symbol of grassroots solidarity. It also spread internationally.

Within four months, we had a 7-day operation, 170 meals a day to around 21 locations. Hot meal packs sent out with other essential hygiene items and items to help with boredom and isolation. We've served 140,000 meals now. We've intercepted over 60 tonnes of food waste from supermarkets, farms, market stores, shops from all over the city.

The App is brilliant [g]. You open it, two or three clicks…and you find a service to support the need you're looking for... It's fast and free. Within a year we have built a team, acquired funding and it has been launched. We now have more than 130 support services approved with incredible information for every single sector, every child, every doctor, every social worker, every teacher, every person walking down the street, anyone who has a friend or family member …It's designed to be a tool to activate the 250,000 people in this city to support another person."

Andrew: From a community cohesion perspective, I have been in discussions with colleagues - we need to recognise and celebrate the contributions of our community volunteers who are our real social capital. For example, those who have made significant contributions to assist other in the most challenging time. Those who put their lives, their time, and their energy to help others in the most difficult time, when peoples were worried what would happen to them and their loved ones. But then there were people, who put themselves forward, knowing that the virus may end their life. But they served us and those who were in need. We must be proud of them...

---

[g] Tony is describing the recent launch of a healthcare support app developed by him and his team. See www.hopeinswansea.org.uk for more information. And see https://shiftdesign.org/case-study-compassionate-frome/ for the story of Compassionate Frome, where local healthcare workers developed a way of supporting people across the their town. For an update, read the talk with 'Hannah' in the Appendix of this book.

31: Choices of Reconstruction

"I understood nothing of that kind of loss - of the crumbling of the physical texture of lives lived, the way the meaning of a place could change because those who used to be in it were no longer there." (62)

Most people's lives are an idiosyncratic, unlikely mulch of things that might not have happened. My childhood was one of living, playing and being raised in Greenhill. And with a rhythm to those days that we took for granted, cossetted, as we were, by an extended local reach that spanned space and time. And leaving home proved to be one of the best decisions I made. It gave access to educational, social and work opportunities and friendships, that I wouldn't otherwise have had. I met many people who changed my life, and opened doors which opened doors.

But leaving didn't turn out to be an event. I found out that you can't leave a place that's in you. And that in my childhood time and place were part of the same thing. As life rolled on, leaving became a negotiation with others and with myself. This was complicated because of the relationships between me and my parents, and of us with ourselves. So full of warmth, love, pain, tearing, anger and chest-crushing inarticulacy. Add to this the certainty that comes with growing older: that time has been playing tricks. It's not linear at all. Time has its own family, and its moments are cousins, waving across a crowded room.

***

"You were asking a personal thing earlier. I think one of the reasons I'm interested to do this book is there was a little bit of me that always felt slightly guilty for leaving."

"No, no you shouldn't", said Tom, feeding his chickens. "It's the way of the world... But really, you're probably feeling a little bit of hiraeth, right. A little bit of the longing."

147

Hiraeth, the word dating back to the very early Welsh records, and meaning a longing for an unattainable person, place or time that can't be revisited. Like the Greek *nostalgia*, the Spanish *sausade*, the Japanese *Mono no aware*, all concerned with the impermanence of the world, one's place in it, and the bitter-sweet impossibility of re-visiting the past.

It took time for the memory-dust to settle. It's clearer to me now that my unease about leaving Greenhill isn't about guilt and regret. It's more about loss. As I became myself, privileged by new opportunities, I lost a shared language and the bond changed with my parents. As the decades passed, I understood better the swirl and significant moments of my parents' lives. The sharper understanding brought clarity and a pain from knowing there was no return journey. This rupture of personal development can be especially severe for people from the working class and isn't mentioned in the university brochures. And it's the conversations we didn't have that last the longest. Though they're gone, my wish would be to spend one day together with my parents, laughing and talking about how we were and who we are. Knowing that would be a comfort gives a consolation of itself.

What surprised me when talking to the people in this book, was just how much they wanted to tell their own story about themselves in Greenhill. What started as a hunch was soon replaced by the obvious truth that this was a place where impressions formed were deep and had lasted a lifetime. As they recalled their memories, people changed. Some became quieter, grateful, humorous, focused, and some became angry, or confused, or bitter. What was clear was the strength of emotional connection to time and place for these people. They were grateful to have an opportunity to articulate what it meant to them.

As the area changed from a place to be, to one to pass, there was a feeling of loss. They'd been there, and knew what it meant. And their memories grated with their present. It felt very personal: the sense of being part of something bigger, which once held you in the pouch of its history. Loss for one's childhood, sure, but much more: the slow forgetting of the location and the meaning of a place, and of the people who lived there, and of a way of living.

**

COVID-19 reminded us of our place. Forced to stay where we live, we spent more time thinking about it. And for more of us that means cities. In 2008, for the first time on our planet, more people lived in cities than in rural areas. In 2020 that figure was 56% and by 2050 is predicted to be 68% of a population of 9.77 billion. Cities are major markets for energy, consuming around 70% of global energy and producing around 75% of global carbon emissions. And the fastest urban population growth will happen in low-income and lower-middle income countries, where resources are tight. It's easy to see why the United Nations predicts that sustainable urban living will become a key challenge of our century. (63)

As Greenhill deals with the challenges of poverty, health, living standards and the environment, it becomes a modern-day test case for sustainable urban living. It's in neither the east nor west, but in the older, central part of the city. A blind spot, avoided by some, ignored by many. Remember that feeling, in the early months of COVID-19, when speaking with that minority of people who'd contracted it? There was a sense of awkwardness, even shame. They'd avoid eye contact, as if they'd done something wrong. Illness, slum clearances and poverty all marginalise, and shame ushers difference to silence.

And there are echoes of its own history. Of how micro-organisms and poverty caused economic decay and ill-health. Of the need for the effective integration of peoples from other parts of the world. Of tensions between precarious working conditions, economic opportunities and environmental health. And of how a place's economy changed, once from agriculture to industry and collectives, now to zero-hour contracts and fragmentation.

Walking through Greenhill now, a stranger would discover very little about its history. But it has a proud one that should be celebrated

149

and there are lessons to learn for sustainable urban living. In becoming an urban neighbourhood, it integrated Welsh and Irish people for more than 100 years in relative harmony. And it did this through building institutions that people wanted, as well as becoming a place for expressing cultural customs that made the area distinctive and the local people proud. It prospered through creating the common aim of being a happy and safe place to live, worship and learn, for Welsh and Irish people.

There was a sufficient diversity of life in the area, such that people could get most of their needs from where they lived. There has been a re-birth of interest in the 20-minute neighbourhood concept: that most of what we need should be accessible within a short walk of home. (64) Greenhill was a 20-minute neighbourhood before the concept existed. Food, drinks, money, support, entertainment, conversation, worship, education, friendship, play, doctors, and more, were all available locally.

And all of this ensured a multitude of social interactions: different strokes for different folks. And these many conversations were the engine of social bond-building, which led to giving and receiving financial, emotional, practical and psychological support. This protected people from the everyday threat of poverty, and made everyday life more safe, more social, more fun.

It was undermined more through ignorance than malign intent. Through ill-considered local decisions, and by impersonal, global forces. Its decline is a cautionary tale that also brings lessons. Housing and road changes undermined the social processes that made the area what it was. Change would have happened anyway, because of wider societal forces, but these local decisions ravaged local relationships and hastened fragmentation. And the siloes of government meant that decisions could be taken by outsiders, with little understanding of how it would affect community life.

A deficit-mindset exists in much government thinking. Resource-pressed local governments tend to move money to problem areas, rather than protecting neighbourhood assets that already exist and contribute to the quality of living. As in healthcare, funds go to treatment of illness, rather than to prevention and the protection of what already works. Who was thinking about the neighbourhood as a whole and understanding the inter-connectedness of the place - how it really 'worked'? In this case, the city government didn't protect a community asset, and only responded when crimes and social ills manifested.

And, perhaps for the people there, it became taken for granted as simple, ordinary 'everyday life'. The safety, friendships and pleasures perhaps became so familiar that we stopped looking to the horizon for threats.

This isn't about matters of change and preservation. Why preserve a way of life that people don't want any more? What matters is what we want about where we live, and how able we consider ourselves to make things happen. The shift to urban living will continue, and many relatively poor neighbourhood places will need local ingenuity. Greenhill is at yet another juncture in its history and the future is open for choices. What might be possible?

***

Since spring 2020 the topic of 'community has summoned our attention. And we've been reminded of the work of people who've been at this for a while. Jane Jacobs thought of cities as living systems, seemingly crammed with random comings and goings, but actually providing a complex order brought to life through places that allowed random meetings to occur. Like Eric Klinenberg, and his work on social infrastructure, Jacobs believed that the frequency and variety of these encounters was key in city spaces. And that diversity was an indispensable feature of vibrant urban life. In her 1958 article in Fortune magazine: "Downtown is For People" and her 1961 book: "The Death and Life of Great American Cities", she argued that cities need diversity. It can bring economic vitality, the capacity for cities to renew themselves, and attract tourists and visitors. People will meet people who bring something different and form partnerships to solve problems that otherwise remain stubbornly fixed:

"Does anyone suppose that, in real life, answers to any of the great questions that worry us today are going to come out of homogenous settlements?" (65)

Jacobs was also an advocate and mobiliser of people, and in the late 1950s, she successfully formed a neighbourhood group to thwart Robert Moses' plans to extend Fifth Avenue through Washington Square Park, in Greenwich Village, through to Broome Street in present day SoHo, Manhattan.

This issue of local agency underpins the *Asset-Based Community Development* work of Cormac Russell. He looks at people living in local places and taking responsibility for each other and their local resources. One of the strengths of Russell's work is that he makes us think about organising at the community level. And about the community assets we already have, and what we did together that made things the way we are.

In Greenhill, most people are unaware of the rich history of the place. Yet the list of community assets is considerable. The area has nearness to the city centre. It takes about 25 minutes to walk from the Spar on Carmarthen Road to the city centre. It has potential for start-up enterprises to build businesses at affordable cost. Transport-wise, it has easy access to the nearby train station and a major road out of the city, towards the M4. There is land adjacent to the railway which could be turned into social, cultural and business units. It hosts an outstanding catholic junior school which attracts a very diverse population, and acts as a feeder to a secondary school. It has a large hall, a separate community centre, and Bryn-Melyn Park, an open green space for play. It contains Swansea's only cathedral, and with historical, archived records that people want. And culturally, it represents a history of Irish and Welsh cultures integrating and living in harmony for over a hundred years, which is embedded in the collective memory.

There are no simple transferable prescriptions for change from elsewhere, because local context and local aims are important. But there are some broad principles that can be the starting point for a meaningful reconstruction.

First, honour the past. With such a rich social, cultural and industrial heritage, the area's story should be told. There is a collective value in archiving stories of people and places and times. St Joseph's school has done this, with its arts project, to help their schoolchildren understand the origins and industrial heritage of the place.

In Lisbon, the old district of Alfama in Lisbon leads up a steep hill to the castle. Walking around the area you'll see plated images of neighbourhood characters attached to walls. People like Gabriela and Sara. And with an explanatory note attached in one spot:

> "The castle is the cradle of Lisbon. In recent times the exodus of its population has taken away the central role which it should never have lost. With this exhibition "Soul of the Castle" the inhabitants move back into the spotlight, receiving recognition for their role in preserving the cultural values that make this neighbourhood unique."

The photos were taken by artist Camilla Watson to capture and honour the history of the area, and the role of specific people. (66) Watson's work started as a voluntary project, got local support, and was eventually founded by the local borough. Greenhill should have a historical museum that showcases the neighbourhood's story, run by local people.

At the same time, most of the stories of Greenhill are old ones. New stories are needed that mean something to the people living and working there now. As with Irish immigration in the 19th century, so the area today welcomes people from elsewhere, only a much more diverse mix. The word *cynefin* fits here. Charlotte Williams shares the Curriculum for Wales description of *cynefin* as 'the historic, cultural and social place which has shaped and continues to shape the community which inhabits it'. (67) And she goes on to dissect the term, noting how in our highly inter-connected and mobile world, meanings of places include, invite and welcome some while excluding, denying and marginalising others. What are all the ways in which a rosy view of the place in the past might not help its people now? As Williams continues, what might be new *routes* to a Welsh citizenship, rather than allowing historical *roots* to determine inclusion? More diversity can make it harder to find common grounds, but a more plural, welcoming view of it is possible with curiosity, will and resources. With opportunities and support, residents and visitors can create their own reasons for being here now.

Pleasurable interactions build the bonds that lead to people meeting again. We're back to the social infrastructure of pavements, shops, libraries, cafes, streets, parks, barbers, bars, community centres, green spaces, roof top common spaces, music venues, shared workspaces and more. These provide opportunities for people to stop, talk, transact, learn, gossip, share and build the social capital and trust that makes a place neighbourly. Not everyone wants the same thing: make sure there are plenty of different ways to meet. Without these places, community-building will not happen. The city council, public-private partnerships and local people should work at creating spaces where people want to gather.

And do bother to ask local people what they want:

> "Over the last 5 decades, however, in the areas of health and well-being, education, local economics, environment, justice, and public safety, the role of community assets has been relegated to second place, treated as irrelevant to the primary concerns of social, political and economic change. Institutions have replaced citizens as the primary inventors of the solutions to social and political problems." (68)

Russell's point is that there has been a growth since the 1990s in institutions becoming the default mechanism for introducing change. Most people don't work in these institutions, and don't believe they have the means to influence them. How people in city institutions and neighbourhoods work together is a key challenge. A similar point is made by Robin Hambleton who points out that

> "Over the last 30 years or so, place-less leaders, that is, people who are not expected to care about the consequences of their decisions for particular places and communities, have gained extraordinary power and influence. This place-less power, which arises largely

155

because of the globalisation of the economy, needs to be challenged." (69)

And it's not just about power and change. People in institutions write accounts of history. They have the authority and resources to do this, along with the channels of access to government, media, police reports, social science surveys, museums and academic research studies. (70) Under pressure of limited resources, and high expectations and evaluation by others, people tend to revert to habit. Taking the time to involve locals in decision-making slows things down. It's easy to see why people in city government decide for themselves. But it's usually a mistake.

The challenge of sustainable urban living can't be left to governments and other institutions. Mainly because they don't have the answers. Also, because putting ideas into action requires working together. Institutional governments can provide money, skills, favourable economic conditions for employment creation; media attention, targets, measurement of change and urgency. Local people care more about those places than people who don't live there. They bring local knowledge of what is treasured, and how to make change happen, through who knows whom and what. A respectful collaboration is our best hope for the collective creativity we need to solve the challenges of sustainable urban living in the coming decades.

Sources

1. Swansea Castle, South Wales Daily News, March 28, 1878 (https://newspapers.library.wales/view/3506281/3506285/101/. Accessed on 30/7/2020
2. Lower Swansea valley: legacy and future, Swansea City Council, Page 7)
3. https://www.dailymail.co.uk/news/article-6866569/Businesses-Swansea-say-shutting-shop-amid-plague-drug-addicts-prostitutes.html
4. https://www.bbc.co.uk/news/uk-wales-57214005 Accessed on 30/5/2019
5. https://www.walesonline.co.uk/news/wales-news/swansea-waun-wen-drugs-crime-22488107 Accessed on 27/9/22
6. Chris Evans, White Rock Copper Works, in 100 Places that Made Britain, 2018. David Musgrove
7. The Wider World, J. R. Alban, in the City of Swansea, Challenges and Change, 1990, Edited by Ralph A. Griffiths, page 126
8. Reminiscences of the early days of the Parish and Church of St Josephs Greenhill Swansea, by the Very Rev. J. W. Richards, OSB, 1919, page 6
9. Dolen Mynyw Menevia News. September 2020. Down memory lane: Father Charles Kavanagh. Page 9. https://www.diocese.cc/FileSystem/11/Public/Publications/9/197/pages.pdf. Accessed 20/9/22
10. The Story of Swansea's districts and villages, 1964, N. L. Thomas, page 121
11. Ibid, page 122
12. Early Catholic days in Swansea. J. D. W., reporting on Father Kavanagh's 1852 annual return to the Bishop of the Diocese.
13. Reminiscences of the early days of the parish and church of St joseph's, Greenhill, Swansea, by the Very Rev J. W. Richards. OSB, 1919, page 7

14. Ibid, pages 8-9
15. Benedictine work at Greenhill, Swansea, The Cambrian, 13th August, 1886, https://newspapers.library.wales/view/3337428/3337433/24/. Accessed on 20/7/2020
16. Reminiscences of the early days of the parish and church of St joseph's, Greenhill, Swansea, by the Very Rev J. W. Richards. OSB, 1919, page 23
17. Corpus Christi celebrations at Swansea. The Cambrian, 30/6/1905: https://newspapers.library.wales/view/3347765/3347767/14/). Accessed on 20/7/2020
18. Swansea. The Herald, 4th December 1915. https://newspapers.library.wales/view/4114967/4114975/178/
19. Outcasts in an outhouse. Cardiff Times, August 10th, 1907. (https://newspapers.library.wales/view/3433595/3433603/198 l/)
20. Greenhill Rowdies, Father Fitzgerald's indignant outburst. The Cambrian, 26th May 1905. (https://newspapers.library.wales/view/3347720/3347722/17/ Greenhill%20And%20riot)
21. Reminiscences of the early days of the parish and church of St joseph's, Greenhill, Swansea, by the Very Rev J. W. Richards. OSB, 1919, page 27
22. The Rorke's Drift Men: Heroes of the Zulu War. 2010 James W. Bancroft.
23. Introduction, John Lorinc, in The Ward: the life and loss of Toronto's first Immigrant neighbourhood. 2015. Edited by John Lorinc, Michael McClelland, Ellen Scheinberg and Tatum Taylor
24. Grieving for a lost home: psychological costs of relocation, Marc Fried. In Urban Renewal, the Record and the Controversy. (1966). Edited by James Q. Wilson. Cambridge, Mass. M.I.T. Press. Page 359
25. Ibid, page 362
26. Identity as place: Constructing a Welsh Identity through nature. Durre Shahwar. I Welsh (Plural): Essays on the Future of Wales.

2022. Edited by Darren Chetty, Grug Muse, Hanan Issa and Iestyn Tyne.

27. Marc Fried, 85; led key study on urban renewal. Boston Globe obituary. http://archive.boston.com/bostonglobe/obituaries/articles/20 08/05/18/marc_fried_85_led_key_study_on_urban_renewal/? page=2. Accessed on 3/4/2021

28. http://www.welshcoalmines.co.uk/GlamWest/Brynlliw.htm

29. Rush to claim coal dust disease money. South Wales Evening Post. October 15th, 1974

30. Office for National Statistics: https://www.ons.gov.uk/employmentandlabourmarket/peoplei nwork/employmentandemployeetypes/datasets/employmentun employmentandeconomicinactivityforpeopleaged16andoveranda gedfrom16to64seasonallyadjusteda02sa

31. It's the sugar that causes all the trouble. South Wales Evening Post. April 20th, 1974

32. Carbon Black: 100 Swansea wives off to No. 10. South Wales Evening Post. April 14th, 1973

33. Typhoid risk epidemic in Gower. South Wales Evening Post. June 22nd, 1971

34. Yellow fever in Swansea, 1986. P.D. Meers. J Hyg (Lond), Volume 97, 185-191

35. Revolution in the Head: The Beatles records the sixties. 1994. Ian MacDonald. Pages 27-28

36. Fly what you like. Woodbine ad – South Wales Evening post. April 1970.

37. Bowling Alone: The Collapse and Revival of American Community. 2000. Robert Puttnam. New York: Simon and Schuster

38. County Highway Authority. Carmarthen Road Public meeting, 13th December 1977. (Archive document, Swansea City Council.)

39. Planning blight-still no end to the residents' 25-year nightmare. South Wales Evening Post. 25th May, 1978

40. Strikes in the UK: withering away? https://www.eurofound.europa.eu/publications/article/1999/strikes-in-the-uk-withering-away Accessed on 12/09/21
41. TV sets hit by repair firm strike. South Wales Evening Post. May 15th, 1976.
42. Anthony Hopkins to quit Britain. South Wales Evening Post. September 24th, 1977.
43. Crisis? What crisis? http://news.bbc.co.uk/1/hi/uk_politics/921524.stm. Accessed 9/9/21
44. British Economy Picture Is Black. South Wales Evening Post. March 3rd, 1980
45. 5,000 behind with their rent. South Wales Evening Post. June 3rd, 1981
46. One Is Six Is Jobless. South Wales Evening Post. September 21st, 1982
47. Red Flu ready to hit Britain. South Wales Evening Post. January 5th, 1979
48. Cutting the Swansea brain drain. South Wales Evening Post. 14th March, 1980
49. Kearns, A. 2003. Social Capital, regeneration and social policy. Quoted on page in 166 in Urban Regeneration in the UK. 2021 by Andrew Tallon. 3rd edition, Routledge
50. The Death and life of Great American Cities. 1961. Jane Jacobs. Page 40
51. Culture is Ordinary. 1958. Raymond Williams.
52. 5 facts about the UK service sector. Office for National Statistics. https://www.ons.gov.uk/economy/economicoutputandproductivity/output/articles/fivefactsabouttheukservicesector/2016-09-29. Accessed on 5/8/2022
53. Making sense of the Knowledge Economy. The Telegraph. https://www.telegraph.co.uk/business/tips-for-the-future/the-knowledge-economy/ Accessed on 5/8/2022

54. CEO of Strathcarron Hospice: https://www.nurturedevelopment.org/blog/people-die-twice/ Accessed on 19/8/2021

55. Palaces For The People: How to Build a More Equal and United Society. 2018. Eric Klinenberg. Page 3

56. Bowling Alone: The Collapse and Revival of American Community. 2000. Robert Puttnam. New York: Simon and Schuster. Page 283

57. The Death and life of Great American Cities. 1961. Jane Jacobs. Page 357

58. Eugenia South et al. Neighbourhood Blight, Stress and Health: A walking trial of Urban Greening and Ambulatory Heart Rate. American Journal of Public health. Vol 105, No 5. 2005

59. The Future Generations Report 2020: Executive Summaries. https://www.futuregenerations.wales/

60. Population report of Swansea Lower Super Output Areas, 2010-2020

61. Joseph Rowntree Foundation. 2nd November 2020. https://www.jrf.org.uk/press/wales-faces-rising-tide-poverty-after-coronavirus

62. The indelible woman: Margaret Atwood on To the Lighthouse https://www.theguardian.com/books/2002/sep/07/classics.margaretatwood Accessed on 3/5/2020

63. 68% of the world population projected to live in urban areas by 2050, says UN. 16th May 2018. https://www.un.org/development/desa/en/news/population/2018-revision-of-world-urbanization-prospects.html. Accessed on 19/05/2021

64. What is a 20-minute neighbourhood? https://www.sustrans.org.uk/our-blog/get-active/2020/in-your-community/what-is-a-20-minute-neighbourhood/ Accessed on 12/04/2022

65. The Death and life of Great American Cities. 1961. Jane Jacobs. Page 584-5

66. Alma de alfama. https://www.camillawatson.com/alma-de-alfamasoul-of-alfama

67. Knowing our place: Cynefin, Curriculum and me. Charlotte Williams. In Welsh (Plural): Essays on the Future of Wales. 2022. Edited by Darren Chetty, Grug Muse, Hanan Issa and Iestyn Tyne. Page 205

68. Rekindling Democracy: A Professional's Guide to Working in Citizen Space. 2020. Cormac Russell. Cascade Books. Page 7

69. Robin Hambleton. Place-based leadership: A new perspective on urban integration. Journal of Urban regeneration and renewal. 2015. Vol 9, page 19

70. Changing the archive. Glenn Jordan and Chris Weedon. In A Tolerant nation? Revisiting Ethnic Diversity In A Devolved Wales. 2015. Edited by Charlotte Williams, Neil Evans and Paul O'Leary

71. https://compassionate-communitiesuk.co.uk/2021/11/28/the-frome-model/ Accessed 12/09/2022

Appendix

Compassionate Communities – The Frome Story

I'd been working in the area of people and learning and collaboration between organisations, and in places like cities. I'd completed my doctorate, looking at how teams of people who were challenged to develop novel ideas went about this. And what were the sorts of conversations that seemed to aid new thinking, and, sometimes, got in the way?

I was part of a team running leadership development courses on this, through the local University of the West of England. In 2011, Hannah was a participant. She was a GP from Frome, a town of around 30,000 people, and she'd noticed that many people were at risk of loneliness and isolation.

In the years following the programme, Hannah worked with a wider team from the same GP practice, and many people from other Somerset hospitals, contract-commissioning organisations, local councils, district nursing, citizens advice and more. They set up the Compassionate Frome project, providing advice on medical well-being, social connections, financial and mental health. Between them they established a community of healthcare professionals as well as volunteers, all of whom helped signpost people to existing health and care services in Frome. The aim was to connect people to what was present, and to reduce the number of people routinely going to accident and emergency at local hospitals. The work has been lauded nationally and internationally, leading to a drop in hospital admissions, and cost savings, while those were rising in the rest of the county. (71)

I'd kept in touch with Hannah as the years had passed, and she'd been typically generous with her time and thoughts. Some of these found their way into conference papers and publications from me and my colleagues. What they'd done had been very innovative, co-ordinating healthcare support across multiple organisations. Hannah is modest and realistic. She sees the success of the work as down to a much wider group of people, though she has sometimes spearheaded it, and taken responsibility for promoting the work publicly. She won a Points of Light award from the UK government. We spoke in October 2020, 7 months into the UK pandemic, about how the work was going, and how COVID had affected it.

We lived in a little village called Nunney for a number of years. And it was just an amazing place where I could have told you who lived up Hall Street, naming each house, as you went all the way up and all the way down. And everybody knew what everybody else was doing. But there was that sense of real solidarity. And, and I had my children there, and there were 13 babies born, the year I had my first daughter. There were 13 young mums all with their first baby all at once. Sort of finding the shell shock of what it was like to be responsible for this small infant. And, you know, it was a real strong sense of, you know, being in it together.

Well, I think it has made those casual interactions much more difficult. But at the same time, I think it has made us much more aware of the value of those interactions…there probably still is a lot of stigma around loneliness, isn't there? If you felt that you were on your own, pre-COVID there can be you know, that psychology that says: 'there must be something wrong with me'. Whereas I think everybody is struggling with it now. And so, that is the kind of levelling effect as well. And I think some of the most isolated people probably felt a little bit less isolated, because everybody was in the same boat. Is it socially acceptable to go somewhere on my own? That's really hard for people, isn't it?

So it had had an effect on reducing the number of people going to their GP, because in a way they were getting support outside of that. How much has that continued into 2020 and lockdown, would you say?

I think it continues. I think the other thing is, it helps clinical teams to talk about what matters most. So, if somebody comes in, and they've got blood pressure, and an infected toe…and it's making their lungs worse, you can have a conversation about those medical things. But it does encourage you and facilitate talking about what's going on in their life, and why they might be getting referrals into that state. So that's been really good. I think the other thing we've done, we've worked really hard for integration and collaboration across the different silos in health and social care. So just as, there was a big focus on trying to support communities to deal with what matters most. And recognising the great assets that were already in the community, that we could draw upon them, and encourage people to be an active citizen in…There's much more of a sense of, we're here for the community in Frome. We try and find the right solution for that individual. And there's much more give and take that comes from that collaborative working, and seeing ourselves as one team rather than several separate teams.

Right at the beginning of lockdown, we were very quickly able to put a list of resources together, because we knew who to ask, and most of the resources, were already in touch with us. So we were able to write out to well-shielded patients and say: these are the, these are the people to get in touch with, this is our telephone number, you can get this by this route, that by the other route. If you've got any problems get in touch. So, largely when we were phoning that vulnerable group, to check they were okay, people's own network of support had rallied around them. And there were very few people who didn't have that personal network of support there.

But I think, that shared vulnerability, that recognition, when we couldn't go swimming on a Thursday morning, or we couldn't go to the market, like we normally did, of how much we miss those things, and the people that you would have said hello to, when you were walking your dog. Those little touches, I think, people generally are much more aware of the importance of those light touch interactions as well as big relationships.

Do you see those happening, those light touches?

We're all trying to have those light touches in ways that are safe and possible. And I think people are having to make much more of an active effort for those things to happen. But I think as a result, we probably will value them a lot more than we did when we took them all for granted. And they didn't even register on our psyche, because that was how life was. We will have a different calibration of what's important.

And you're always telling me, of course, it's not just you. And we all know that, although sometimes we make heroes, don't we, out of individuals, in retrospect?

And that's a miserable thing to do, because we are a strong community in Frome...And it definitely wasn't me that set everything up. It's just that - who was our community development worker, was able to map everything out. And we were able to integrate it into primary care so that it's embedded in what we do...So having a database now, with the health connections website, where you can tell people exactly where things are, and make suggestions is really liberating for my work, certainly. And, and the great success is when you have a conversation with someone and they say: well, I was thinking of getting in touch with my sister and doing this, that and the other. And actually, all you're doing is having a conversation and reflecting back to them, the solutions that they've got there already and trying to help them to actually put those in place. We all know ourselves really well. We all have a support network around us. But sometimes we forget to access that, or we don't feel sufficiently important or sufficiently interesting, or whatever it might be, to feel that we won't bother them. And yet, when you do, people are really pleased that you have. They're touched! They're interested in you. They're the people that cared about you, which is why they are your network of support.

Milton Keynes UK
Ingram Content Group UK Ltd.
UKHW021814121123
432434UK00010B/80